Fort Dodge

Grenville Mellen Dodge, 1831–1916, native of Massachusetts, was trained as a civil engineer and became a railroad construction contractor in Iowa in the 1850s. When the Civil War interrupted railroad building, Dodge was commissioned colonel of the Fourth Iowa Infantry. He fought in Missouri and Arkansas and distinguished himself at Pea Ridge, where three horses were shot from under him and he was wounded. For his gallantry Dodge was promoted to brigadier general of volunteers in 1862. He then commanded the District of Mississippi, oversaw railroad construction there, organized black regiments for Union service, and was an important officer during the Vicksburg campaign, after which he was promoted to major general of volunteers. He was severely wounded at the siege of Atlanta in August 1864. In December 1864 he was sent west to command the Department of the Missouri, where he directed a campaign against hostile Indians in 1865. He ordered the establishment of several new military posts, including Fort Dodge (named to honor him), to help protect overland trails and projected railroads across the Plains. In January 1866 the department was reorganized and command was given to General John Pope. General Dodge resigned from the army in May 1866 to supervise construction of the Union Pacific Railroad. After completion of the transcontinental connection in 1869, Dodge built railroads in the Southwest and later in Cuba. After retirement in 1903 he was a popular lecturer on the Civil War and railroads. His home in Council Bluffs, Iowa, is a national landmark. Fort Dodge and Dodge City immortalize this soldier and pioneer railroad construction engineer.

Fort Dodge
Sentry of the Western Plains

by Leo E. Oliva

Kansas State Historical Society
Topeka, Kansas

THE AUTHOR: Dr. Leo E. Oliva is a former university professor of history. He farms with his wife, Bonita, in Rooks County, Kansas, and is the owner of Western Books publishing company. In addition Oliva is a freelance historian whose writing and research has focused on the frontier army and Indians as well as local history. This book is the fifth in the Kansas Forts Series. Oliva's other publications include *Soldiers on the Santa Fe Trail* (1967), *Ash Rock and the Stone Church: The History of a Kansas Rural Community* (1983), and *Fort Union and the Frontier Army in the Southwest* (1993).

FRONT COVER: *Moving On*, Fort Dodge, Kansas, 1865–1882, by Jerry D. Thomas. Thomas, a nationally acclaimed artist, has made a career of creating wildlife and western art. His original works will appear on the covers of all eight volumes of the Kansas Forts Series. Thomas is a resident of Manhattan, Kansas.

Fort Dodge: Sentry of the Western Plains is the fifth volume in the Kansas Forts Series published by the Kansas State Historical Society in cooperation with the Kansas Forts Network.

Additional Works in the Kansas Forts Series:
Fort Harker: Defending the Journey West
Fort Hays: Keeping Peace on the Plains
Fort Larned: Guardian of the Santa Fe Trail
Fort Leavenworth: Gateway to the West
Fort Riley: Citadel of the Frontier West
Fort Scott: Courage and Conflict on the Border
Fort Wallace: Sentinel on the Smoky Hill Trail

Second printing 2003

Library of Congress Card Catalog Number 98-86546

ISBN 0-87726-049-4

Printed by Mennonite Press, Inc., Newton, Kansas

CONTENTS

FOREWORD

Fort Dodge is the fifth in the Kansas Forts Network series sponsored by the Kansas State Historical Society. The emphasis is on an analysis of the military responsibilities of the fort but also covered is the daily life of the soldier and the conditions of service.

The choice of location of Fort Dodge in the spring of 1865 was considered at the time a temporary expediency and militarily weak because of the bluffs overlooking the encampment. The low, poorly drained bottom ground was judged by early post surgeons to be a hazard to health. Major General Philip H. Sheridan's survey in 1868 noted the scarcity of wood and reported the land in the vicinity was sterile and infertile. Once established, the dictates of time and budget prevented relocating to a more favorable site. The post, however, was to serve well the military assignments given until 1882 when, after a peacetime interlude of indecision and the disposal of most of the reservation lands, the remaining facilities were converted to the Kansas State Soldiers' Home and continues in that capacity to this day.

The original location near the junction of the Wet Route and the Dry Route of the Santa Fe Trail, determined that the first assignment would be to protect travel and trade on the trail. As conditions became more volatile, maintaining a tenuous balance of status quo between Indians and white settlers and traders required on occasion a showing of military force. After 1865 this frustrating assignment shifted to serving as the major supplier of the army in the field during the Indian wars.

Daily life regardless of the fort's role was "generally routine, monotonous, and austere." Although the poorly paid trooper's life was marked by desertion, drunkenness, and drudgery, when called on the men acted with courage and military competence. The dire predictions caused by the fort's mislocation proved to be unwarranted, even the men's health bore no extraordinary ill effects. The troops suffered only one major epidemic that swept all of the Plains in the summer of 1867.

In this well-researched yet concise accounting of a western military post, Leo Oliva has presented a fascinating story of the role that the people connected with Fort Dodge played in the white settlement of southwestern Kansas.

C. Robert Haywood
Emeritus Professor of History
Washburn University

Introduction

Fort Dodge was established in the spring of 1865 on the Santa Fe Trail primarily to help control the Indian tribes in the area. The principal mission was to protect travelers, stagecoaches, stage stations, and pioneer settlers in the region between Fort Larned, sixty miles to the northeast, and Fort Lyon, nearly 160 miles to the west in Colorado Territory.

It was part of a network of frontier forts founded on the overland routes across the Plains to protect the trails and later the construction and operation of railroads and the settlements that developed. After the railroad reached Dodge City on the edge of the military reservation in 1872, Fort Dodge had a close relationship with that notorious frontier town. The post was an important point in the system of supplies for troops in the field and at other military posts during campaigns against Indians.

The soldiers stationed at Fort Dodge were charged with the difficult task of keeping the peace insofar as possible. When hostilities occurred, the troops were authorized to use force sufficient to restore peace. In good time the army was expected to help remove Indians from the area so white settlers could develop farms, ranches, and towns. The army did not achieve that goal alone. A combination of factors, including railroads, buffalo hunters, and settlers, forced the Indians from their homelands.

The army's arduous task of subduing the Indians and opening their lands for permanent white settlement was encumbered by citizens who demanded protection, journalists and pundits who wanted the Indians annihilated, a Congress that expected results without appropriating sufficient funds, and a division of administration of Indian affairs between two government departments. The army was chronically shorthanded and inadequately equipped for the assignment.

Soldiering was not a popular profession, and the ranks were mainly occupied with recent immigrants and unemployed laborers. Recruits willing to serve five years were hard to find and more difficult to keep. The pay was low, living conditions at most frontier posts were bad, and discipline was severe. Soldiers spent much time at hard labor and standing guard. The provisions, clothing, and equipment left over from the Civil War, regardless of condition, were utilized by the army for the next decade. Drunkenness was a serious problem among officers and enlisted men. Most regiments were seldom if ever filled to authorized capacity, and desertion was a perennial problem.

Other problems existed. Federal policy toward Indians was divided between the U.S. Army in the War Department and the Bureau of Indian Affairs in the Department of the Interior. Soldiers and Indians both were perplexed as government policy alternated between the use of force and efforts at peaceful negotiations. Periodically peace councils were conducted and treaties were signed. During those times the army was held in check until hostilities broke out again.

The Indians were not all of one mind either, and some individuals and groups in various tribes wanted peace while others of the same tribes were for war. Many army officers and some enlisted men were frustrated because it was impossible to distinguish between peaceful and hostile Indians. The latter were able to practice a form of hit-and-run warfare that made it virtually impossible to locate and punish the offenders. It was not uncommon to punish the innocent. When innocent victims on both sides were punished for what the other side considered brazen acts of violence or intimidation, the pressures for open warfare were escalated. Keeping the peace was sometimes impossible, given the conflict of cultures and the contest for land, and challenged the best efforts of the officers and soldiers at the frontier forts. In spite of the impediments, the military helped settle the nation's "Indian problem."

Fort Dodge, as were most frontier posts, was abandoned a few years after the Indian presence in the region was eliminated. Unlike the other abandoned posts, which were either occupied or dismantled by civilians, Fort Dodge buildings and a portion of the military reservation were later turned over to the State of Kansas to establish the state soldiers' home in 1890. It has served that mission to the present. The medical history of the post and the soldiers' home form an important part of Fort Dodge history. Initially, however, its history was dominated by Indian–white relations along the Santa Fe Trail.

1

The Santa Fe Trail

The Santa Fe Trail was opened for commercial trade between the United States and Mexico in 1821. Much of the route had been used by Indians long before William Becknell and five companions took a pack train of commodities from the new state of Missouri to Santa Fe in the autumn of that year. It was a propitious time, for Mexico had just achieved independence from Spain, which had kept the borders closed to foreign commerce. The New Mexicans welcomed trade with the United States. Other traders arrived soon after Becknell. It was clear that profits could be made supplying the isolated New Mexicans with cloth, iron tools, Yankee notions, and other manufactured merchandise. In return Mexico could provide gold, silver, furs, mules, donkeys, and, later, wool. In 1822 Becknell took three wagons over the developing Santa Fe Trail. Other traders followed Becknell, including merchants from Mexico, and the commerce grew in value and importance.

The trail affected the economies and cultures of three societies: the Hispanic-Americans of northern Mexico, the Anglo-Americans of the United States, and the Plains Indians through whose lands it passed. Slowly the Anglo-Americans established dominance in New Mexico and forced the Plains Indians onto reservations in present Oklahoma. Several routes of the Santa Fe Trail network developed over the years. All required a supply of water, grass, and fuel sufficient for the movement of wagon trains, which traveled approximately fifteen miles per day.

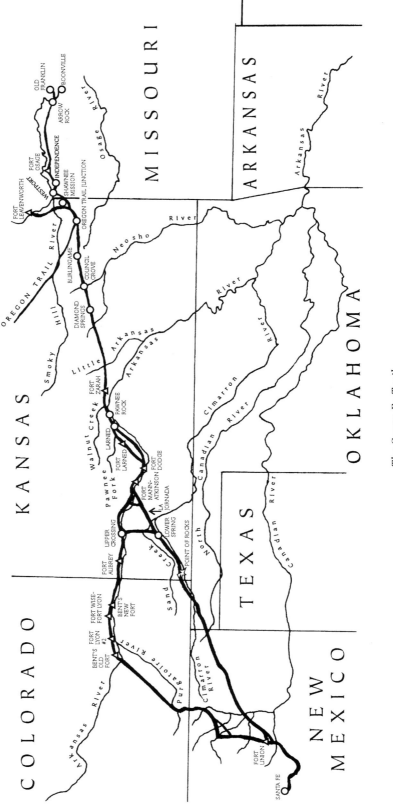

The Santa Fe Trail

Sketch of a wagon train on the Santa Fe Trail, from Josiah Gregg's Commerce of the Prairies *(1844), showing modes and methods of travel between Missouri and northern Mexico.*

There were a number of eastern points of departure and return, including Franklin, Independence, and Westport in Missouri, and Fort Leavenworth in what became Kansas. The wagons often gathered at Council Grove to organize into caravans for mutual protection during the westward trip across the plains. The travelers elected officers, established a system of guards, and agreed on rules for safety and governance. Eastbound wagon trains usually organized in a similar manner at the junction of the Mora and Sapello Rivers, the present town of Watrous in New Mexico, and ceased such paramilitary organization at Council Grove.

Travelers going west joined the Arkansas River at present Ellinwood, Kansas, and followed the north bank of that stream southwestward to Pawnee Rock. West of that famous landmark the trail divided into a Wet Route and Dry Route, the former following closely along the Arkansas River and the latter following a high ridge several miles north of the river. Freighters believed the Dry Route was shorter, although there was actually little difference in the length, because they usually made better time on it. A campground developed just west of where the two routes rejoined, and this site was later selected for the location of Fort Dodge.

3

Francois Xavier Aubry, 1824–1854, a French-Canadian from Quebec, moved to St. Louis in 1843 and worked for a mercantile firm that supplied Santa Fe traders. In 1846 he entered the trade with New Mexico and soon became one of the leading merchants on the trail. During 1847–1848 he made three record horseback rides between Santa Fe and Independence (the fastest trip in five days and sixteen hours). He was the first to take wagons across the Plains several times each year and in 1851 laid out the Aubry Route, considered the best wagon road between the Arkansas River and the Cimarron Route. In 1854 he was killed in a barroom fight in Santa Fe. His name was used to designate the Aubry Route or Aubry Trail, Aubry Spring located about two miles west of Aubry Crossing of the Arkansas River, and Fort Aubrey near Aubry Spring. A Missouri River steamboat was named F.X. Aubry, and towns named Aubry were founded in Missouri, Kansas, Oklahoma, Texas, and Arizona.

During the first quarter century of its use, the main route of the Santa Fe Trail crossed the Arkansas at some point west of the junction of the Wet and Dry Routes, most often at one of the several middle crossings near present Cimarron and Ingalls, Kansas, or the upper crossing near present Lakin, Kansas. The travelers crossed to the Cimarron River, going nearly sixty miles over a "desert" with no reliable source of surface water. The route followed the Cimarron valley from Lower Cimarron Spring (later Wagonbed Spring), south of present Ulysses, across the present Oklahoma panhandle. This route, later known as the Cimarron Route, crossed into New Mexico and followed a road to the crossing of the Canadian River, passed the famous landmark Wagon Mound, to the junction of the Mora and Sapello Rivers at present Watrous. From there the trail wound through the southern Sange de Cristo Mountains, crossed the Pecos River, and climbed over Glorieta Pass into Santa Fe. Some traders

4

Stagecoaches carried mail and passengers between Missouri and New Mexico beginning in 1849, and from the end of track to Santa Fe as the railroads built westward after the Civil War. Mail coaches were sometimes objects of Indian raids. Soldiers stationed at the posts along the overland routes provided protection for stage stations and escorts for the coaches during times of severe threats.

continued south on the Camino Real or Chihuahua Trail into other Mexican states.

Later, in the 1840s, the Mountain Route of the trail developed, following the north bank of the Arkansas River to Bent's Fort near present La Junta, Colorado. Travelers forded the river west of that famous trading post and crossed over Raton Pass, connecting with the Cimarron Route at the Mora and Sapello Rivers. The Mountain Route was longer than the Cimarron Route, and it was difficult for wagon traffic because of rugged Raton Pass. In time improvements were made by the army and civilians to facilitate that passage.

In the early 1850s Francis X. Aubry established another route between the Arkansas River and the Cimarron Route in present Oklahoma. The Aubry Route crossed the Arkansas at Aubry Crossing, east of the present town of Syracuse in western Kansas, and followed a natural road with adequate resources south-southwest through portions

The Santa Fe Trail gave way to the railroad, which made possible more rapid and less expensive shipment of commodities across the Great Plains. The army protected construction and operation of the railroads. The Atchison, Topeka and Santa Fe reached Dodge City, founded on the western edge of the Fort Dodge military reservation, in 1872. Thereafter military supplies came to Fort Dodge by rail. The railroad brought buffalo hunters, cattle drovers, farmers, ranchers, and town builders to the region, all of whom combined with the army to force Indians from the lands of western Kansas.

of present Kansas and Colorado to join the Cimarron Route near Cold Springs in the present Oklahoma Panhandle.

During the Civil War stagecoach service on the Santa Fe Trail shifted from the Cimarron to the Mountain Route. After the Civil War, Richens Lacy (Uncle Dick) Wootton made major improvements and established a toll road over Raton. The railroad built over Raton Pass in 1879 and replaced the last portion of the old Santa Fe Trail when it reached Santa Fe the following year.

As commerce increased over the Santa Fe Trail during and after the 1820s, Indian contacts increased as the tribesmen took advantage of opportunities to trade and plunder. Conflict seemed inevitable. In 1828 Indians killed three of the traders, and merchants engaged in the trade requested troops from the federal government. Military protection in the form of occasional escorts, beginning in 1829, were inadequate because the international boundary was the Arkansas River. The United States and Mexico were unable to work out a plan of mutual protection for the trade. The traders found it necessary to band together into caravans, utilizing a structured paramilitary organization with enough well-armed men to protect themselves.

The trail was a route of conquest during the Mexican War, 1846–1848, when Brigadier General Stephen W. Kearny's Army of the West marched from Fort Leavenworth via Bent's Fort to occupy Santa Fe. This placed the entire trail within the United States, making more effective military protection possible. It was also necessary because an increase in military freighting and civilian commerce, and the establishment of stagecoach service on the route, met expanded Indian resistance. The first military post on the trail, Fort Mann, was established in 1846 a few miles west of the site of later Fort Dodge, primarily as a safe haven and repair station in the midst of hostile Indian country. It had a small garrison that could barely defend itself, and the post was abandoned the following year. Because of Indian troubles, a special unit of Missouri volunteers, commonly known as the Indian Battalion under command of Major William Gilpin, reoccupied Fort Mann and helped safeguard the trail until their term of service expired in 1848.

Regular stagecoach service began in 1849 with a monthly schedule. By 1858 stages were running on a weekly schedule. Additional military posts helped guard the stage lines and other travelers. These included Fort Atkinson, established in 1851 about a mile from the site of Fort Mann; Fort Union, 1851, in New Mexico near the juncture of the Cimarron and Mountain Routes; Fort Larned, 1859, on Pawnee Fork in central Kansas Territory; Fort Wise (later Fort Lyon), 1860, near Bent's New Fort in present Colorado; Fort Zarah, 1864, on Walnut Creek in central Kansas; and in 1865 Camp Nichols in the present Oklahoma Panhandle, Fort Aubrey in far western Kansas, and Fort Dodge. These posts and the soldiers garrisoned at and supplied by them faced Indians who occupied the region and resisted the intrusions on their lands.

2

Plains Indians

ort Dodge was established and existed because of the presence of Indians whose homelands and hunting grounds had been penetrated by westward-moving merchants, soldiers, miners, ranchers, farmers, town builders, preachers, lawyers, editors, saloonkeepers, gamblers, whores, outlaws, and the trails and railroads they followed. Even though the Plains tribes were overwhelmingly outnumbered and technologically deficient in comparison with the emigrants and the U.S. Army, they did not surrender their lands and traditional ways of life without fighting back.

The Indians were defending their families, economic base, and culture. The Euro-Americans, on the other hand, viewed Indian resistance as thievery, savagery, and murder. The Indians held similar views of the intruders on their lands. Neither side understood nor appreciated the culture of the other, making accommodation virtually impossible as long as the Indians held the land the Euro-Americans wanted. Under these circumstances, warfare was probably inevitable. In the long run, given the relative population and technology, the outcome also was inevitable. It was achieved with considerable loss of property and lives on both sides.

Several tribes were residing in or hunting buffalo in the region crossed by the Santa Fe Trail. The Kansa and Osage tribes were located along the eastern portion of the trail. They periodically hunted farther west. Both tribes signed treaties in 1825, granting their permission for the use of the Santa Fe Trail. Pawnees, whose homes were in present

Sioux Chief Pawnee Killer, shown with two of his warriors, meeting with Lieutenant Colenel George A. Custer and a subaltern in 1867. Pawnee Killer tried to prevent General W.S. Hancock from moving troops near the village on Pawnee Fork. He continued to oppose troops, travelers, and settlers in the region between the Platte and Arkansas Rivers and was Custer's nemesis during Custer's ill-fated campaign that was part of "Hancock's War." Pawnee Killer fought at Beecher Island in September 1868 and was at the Battle of Summit Springs in July 1869. He later accepted reservation life at the Red Cloud Agency, Nebraska.

Nebraska and northern Kansas, came south to hunt and raid along the route. They were usually as threatening to other tribes in the area as to Euro-Americans.

The southern bands of the Cheyenne and Arapaho tribes were located north of the Arkansas River in present western Kansas and eastern

Santank (Sitting Bear) was a war leader of the Kiowa tribe, bringing opposition to civilians and soldiers along the Santa Fe Trail during the 1850s and 1860s. Although he signed the Medicine Lodge Treaty in 1868, he, along with Satanta and Big Tree, led an attack on the Warren wagon train in Texas in 1871. They were arrested, and Satank was shot while attempting to escape.

Cheyenne Chief Little Robe was, with Black Kettle, a leader of the peace faction of his tribe. He signed the Medicine Lodge Treaty in 1868, survived Custer's attack at the Washita, and continued to work for peace. He took no part in the Red River War and died on the reservation in 1875.

Colorado. Some of the Lakota Sioux from the Northern Plains periodically came into the same region to hunt. Bent's Fort was established in the early 1830s on the Arkansas River near present La Junta, Colorado, to engage in trade with Indians of the area, especially Cheyennes and Arapahos. Comanches, Kiowas, and Plains Apaches (also called Kiowa Apaches because of their close alliance with the Kiowas), resided mainly to the south of the Arkansas but traveled north of the river to hunt and raid. Farther west, in eastern New Mexico, the Jicarilla Apaches and Moache Utes hunted on the plains from their mountain homes and raided along the Santa Fe Trail.

The buffalo–horse culture of those tribal Americans was a recent development in the long history of people known as Indians, whose ancestors had migrated to North America more than twelve thousand years ago. A succession of cultures had periodically occupied the Great

Kiowa Chief Kicking Bird, cousin of Stumbling Bear, met with General W.S. Hancock at Fort Dodge in 1867. Kicking Bird signed the Little Arkansas and Medicine Lodge treaties and was a leader of the peace faction of his tribe thereafter. He remained on the reservation during the Red River War and was designated head chief of the Kiowas. Some Kiowas thought him a coward and, to prove his courage, Kicking Bird led and won a raid in Texas. He died on the reservation in 1875, possibly poisoned.

Kiowa Chief Stumbling Bear, a cousin of Kicking Bird, met with General W.S. Hancock at Fort Dodge in 1867. Unlike Kicking Bird, Sumbling Bear was a war leader who opposed peaceful accommodation until 1872 when he joined the peace faction. It was claimed that Stumbling Bear was involved in almost every Kiowa battle from 1850 to 1872. He led charges against Kit Carson's troops at the Battle of Adobe Walls in 1864, signed the Medicine Lodge Treaty, and reportedly became an advocate for peace after a military surgeon saved the life of his young son. He died on the reservation in 1903.

Plains. As some groups migrated from other regions, they pushed out those who had come before. The Euro-Americans were the last to claim the country successfully.

The Plains tribes did not surrender peacefully. Warfare, particularly raiding and stealing horses, was a central feature of tribal cultures. Courage and bravery in battle became the highest virtues, and from an early age men were trained to fight as well as hunt. They were considered by many observers to be the finest horsemen in the world and developed well the skills of hit-and-run raiding and the decoy-ambush tactic. They

Tipis were the mobile homes of Plains Indians, being easily erected, taken down, and moved from place to place. Originally covered with buffalo hides, most tipis were covered with canvas after it was available through trade with Euro-Americans.

were prepared to resist outsiders who penetrated their hunting grounds, especially since they were familiar with the terrain. They were defeated, however, by superior technology and overwhelming numbers.

Plains Indians hunted near the Santa Fe Trail, and some came to the trail to raid wagon trains, particularly those that were small or not well protected. Even though Indians raided in small bands, they were virtually impossible to find by troops sent to deal with them. Later, when they saw their continued life on the Plains seriously threatened by the intruders, Cheyennes, Arapahos, Comanches, and Kiowas fought back with a vengeance. Fort Dodge and the other posts on the Plains were founded to counter and, in time, eradicate that resistance.

Indian–white relations on the Plains deteriorated dramatically during the Civil War era, and Indian resistance along routes of travel became intense. In 1864 Indian–white relations on the Plains became increas-

The Plains tribes retaliated against outsiders who came into their homelands and utilized resources necessary to Indian ways of life. They raided travelers and settlers, resulting in an increase in military presence in the region.

ingly violent. The perennial problem of determining who of the tribesmen were hostile and who were friendly produced fatal consequences in that year. In April, in Colorado Territory, Indians reportedly stole approximately 175 head of livestock from a government contract freighter. It was later claimed that the stock had wandered away. The territorial government and troops in Colorado were determined to punish Indians. Lieutenants George S. Eayre and Clark Dunn were sent from Camp Weld near Denver to recover the cattle and punish the thieves. Eayre led troops against some Cheyennes who were not involved. Dunn attacked a band of Cheyenne Dog Soldiers who also were innocent. Lieutenant Eayre later attacked a Cheyenne camp near Fort Larned. Other soldiers attacked Cheyenne camps along the Platte River. In all instances the soldiers were the aggressors. The Cheyennes, not understanding why they were being attacked, retaliated. Members of other tribes joined in the action. Soon marauding bands of warriors raided along all routes across the Central Plains. By mid-summer travel was virtually halted on most of the trails.

Christopher H. (Kit) Carson, 1809–1868, first traveled the Santa Fe Trail in 1826. He became a mountainman and guide, gaining fame for leading John C. Frémont to Oregon and California. He also helped lead General Stephen Watts Kearny from New Mexico to California during the Mexican War. Carson later settled in New Mexico and served as an Indian agent. During the Civil War he was appointed colonel of the First New Mexico Volunteer Infantry and rose to the rank of brigadier general of volunteers. He fought against Indians in the Southwest and on the Plains. He visited Fort Dodge in 1865, following the treaty negotiations at the mouth of the Little Arkansas River (present Wichita, Kansas)

Troops were sent from Fort Riley to protect travelers and punish the Indians. They could not find the Indians, but they reopened the lines of travel. Forts Ellsworth (later Harker) and Zarah were founded to help. Additional forts, including what became Fort Dodge, were planned. More troops were brought to the region in August to find and punish the Indians, without success. The Indians could not be found. These soldiers were withdrawn early in the autumn to go to eastern Kansas to help repulse Confederate General Sterling Price's drive to capture Kansas City and Fort Leavenworth.

Meanwhile some Cheyennes and Arapahos wanted to avoid war and sought to make peace. Cheyenne Chief Black Kettle and other peace chiefs met with government officials near Denver to proclaim their desire for peace. They were sent to camp north of Fort Lyon until peace could be made. There, on Sand Creek, they were attacked on November 29, 1864, by Colonel John M. Chivington and his Third Colorado Cavalry. Although the Indians raised a white flag, men, women, and children were indiscriminately slaughtered and mutilated.

The Sand Creek Massacre increased tensions throughout the Plains, and the blatant attack was condemned by government officials. Relations were also inflamed to the south where Brigadier General Kit Carson attacked a Kiowa village near Adobe Walls on the Canadian River on November 25, 1864. After a fierce engagement, in which the soldiers were saved by their howitzers, Carson captured and destroyed the village.

In anticipation of renewed Indian hostilities the following spring, Major General Grenville M. Dodge was appointed in December 1864 to command the reorganized Department of the Missouri, which included Kansas and the territories of Colorado, Nebraska, and Utah. Dodge learned that Indians had killed nearly two hundred settlers and travelers in Kansas during 1864. He discovered that some licensed Indian traders were supplying the Indians with modern arms and ammunition and quickly revoked the permits to trade.

Dodge recommended additional military posts. Soon Forts Hays and Wallace were established on the Smoky Hill Trail, and Camp Nichols, Fort Aubrey, and Fort Dodge were added to protect the Santa Fe Trail and its environs. This increased military presence may have helped, for most Indian raiding in 1865 was along the Platte Route to the north. Military expeditions were directed toward Indians north of the Platte and south of the Arkansas. Little was accomplished and, following the close of the Civil War, a new peace initiative was launched by the federal government. In October 1865 a few leaders of the tribes who claimed western Kansas as their homeland accepted the terms of the treaties of the Little Arkansas, by which they agreed to leave their homelands and settle on assigned reservations south of the Arkansas River.

Many tribal leaders, however, did not sign or accept the terms of these agreements. These factions vowed to fight to retain their lands. They continued to oppose westward migration at nearly every opportunity until they eventually were crushed into submission by the army and the onrush of Euro-Americans who built railroads, slaughtered the buffalo, and established settlements. Fort Dodge, located on the Santa Fe Trail, was a part of that conquest.

16

3

The Founding of Fort Dodge

Fort Dodge was established in the spring of 1865 as part of the expanded military presence along the overland trails. On March 23, 1865, General Grenville M. Dodge wrote to Colonel James H. Ford, commanding the District of the Upper Arkansas, to propose establishment of a new military post on the Santa Fe Trail west of Fort Larned. On March 28 Colonel Ford, with an escort and Henry Bradley as guide, left Fort Larned to select the site for the new post. A heavy snow forced the party to return to Larned the next day.

On March 30 Colonel Ford directed Captain Henry Pearce, Eleventh Kansas Cavalry, to take two companies from Fort Larned, select a site near old Fort Atkinson, and establish a new post to be called Fort Wagoner. The following day Ford changed the orders, directing that the post be established several miles east of old Fort Atkinson, and that it be named Fort Dodge to honor General Dodge.

The site chosen was the old camping ground for wagon trains traveling the Santa Fe Trail, just west of the western junction of the Wet Route and Dry Route. A stage station, Adkin's Ranch, established at the site in 1863 had been seized and burned by Indians sometime in 1864. The fact that two earlier military posts had been established in the area indicated it was considered a strategic place for dealing with Indians.

The location for the new fort was important because of its proximity to the Wet and Dry Routes and because the major Santa Fe Trail cross-

17

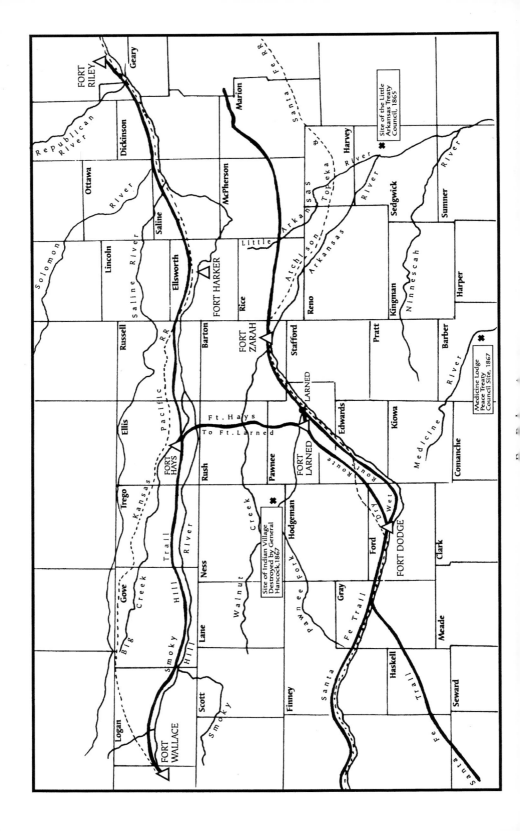

Colorado artist Otto Kuhler created this view of early Fort Dodge to accompany an article by author Leo E. Oliva in 1960 and presented the original sketch to the author. His rendition of Fort Dodge was based on early descriptions and illustrations of the post.

ing of the Arkansas River—the much-used middle or Cimarron Crossing—was some twenty-five miles to the west. The post was situated to provide travelers and traders with a safe stopping place between Forts Larned and Lyon. Troops stationed at the new post also would be available to assist along the Cimarron Route. The garrison could provide escorts for stagecoaches and wagon trains during times of Indian threats.

On April 6, 1865, Captain Pearce with his Company C, Eleventh Kansas Cavalry, and Company F, Second U.S. Volunteer Infantry, departed Fort Larned, and they occupied the new site and established Fort Dodge on April 10. The troops were quartered in tents while dugouts were prepared along the banks of the Arkansas River, and the soldiers lived in dugouts and tents until permanent quarters were constructed in 1867.

Plans were made almost immediately after founding the post to build quarters for the troops. These efforts were probably due more to the trou-

A sketch of the sod officers' quarters at Fort Dodge that appeared in Harper's New Monthly Magazine, *June 1869.*

bles experienced in the use of tents than to any idea of the permanency of the post. The prevailing high winds of the region made living in tents difficult and highly undesirable. As quickly as possible the troops built and occupied dugouts. The river bank was from eight to twelve feet above the water, but the floors were often damp. Also, the dugouts were undoubtedly susceptible to periodic flooding.

Until the summer of 1866, when lumber was received at the post, blankets and gunny-sacks were used to cover the openings left for windows and doorways. Each dugout could accommodate three to four men, and approximately seventy of them were built along the river bank. When lumber arrived in 1866 the dugouts were improved. The soldiers still looked forward to moving out of the holes in the ground into conventional barracks.

The officers' quarters were built of sod above ground. Three were constructed in 1865, each about fourteen by twenty feet and containing one large room. They were located to the north of the dugouts near the center of the long line of quarters in the river bank. A sod kitchen and mess house, 16 by 30 feet, a sod storehouse for quartermaster and commissary supplies, 180 by 20 feet, and a sod hospital, 14 by 40 feet, were also completed in 1865. Dugouts along the river bank, similar to those occupied by the troops, only larger, served as stables for the cavalry horses during the winter of 1865–1866. The quartermaster's stock had to

This sketch of Fort Dodge under construction, titled Interior of Fort Dodge, *by Theodore R. Davis, appeared in* Harper's Weekly, *May 25, 1867.*

remain outdoors during that winter because the quartermaster stables were not completed.

The winter of 1865–1866 was severe, with several blizzards, high winds, and cold temperatures. The men suffered in their humble quarters, with a meager supply of firewood. For a time the post was isolated because the storms shut down traffic on the trail. General Dodge later mused that the post had been named for him in derision by the forsaken soldiers who blamed him for their suffering during that terrible winter in austere dugouts. Desertions likely would have been common if the men had known of a safe place to go and had some way to get there.

Even though the soldiers spent most of their time during the first year constructing quarters and other necessary buildings, the facilities were inadequate to the needs of the garrison. In April 1866 the post commander, Captain George A. Gordon, Second Cavalry, reported to Department Commander John Pope that quarters were insufficient and requested permission to begin construction of suitable barracks immediately. General Pope approved the request, stating that the new structures must be built of materials afforded by the country and the labor was to be performed by the troops. Sod appeared to be the only material available. The attempt to build a large sod stable for cavalry horses ended in failure. The walls bulged in many places and the building collapsed from its own weight before the

21

roof was completed. The spring rains damaged some of the other sod buildings, convincing everyone that sod was not a suitable building material.

A stone quarry was discovered about five miles from the post in June 1866, and plans were made to utilize that material for construction of new buildings. Permission was obtained from General Pope to hire laborers and stonemasons to do the work, with the assistance of soldiers. The

Fort Dodge, 1867. The buildings were not identi-fied. Older sod structures are at left and right, with new construction in the center.

Enlisted men's barracks at Fort Dodge. Two of these structures were of built stone and the other was adobe construction.

Fort Dodge hospital, second from left, and officers' quarters. The commanding officer's quarters is the tallest structure, third from right.

following month four laborers were hired and a foundation was laid for a company barracks. Civilian employees apparently were permitted to construct dugouts along the river for their quarters.

During August twenty more men were hired, and a quarry of better stone was discovered about twelve miles from the post. During that month Captain Gordon was transferred from the post, and the post quartermas-

Fort Dodge commanding officer's quarters, April 1879. The people have not been identified but probably were officers and their families at the post (except the enlisted man holding the pony). Captain James H. Bradford, Nineteenth Infantry, was commanding officer at the time.

ter, Lieutenant George Henry Wallace, Third Infantry, became temporary commander. He decided that a storehouse for the quartermaster stores was of prime importance, and work on the barracks was halted and a storehouse was built. This undoubtedly irritated the troops who anticipated getting out of the uncomfortable dugouts. The quartermaster saw the situation differently, for a considerable portion of the post's supplies had been lost to the elements during the preceding months.

In late November the work of construction was halted for the winter. A quartermaster's storehouse and bakery had been completed and a barracks and hospital started. During the winter of 1866–1867 the laborers were employed in cutting stone to resume construction the following spring.

Throughout the working season of 1867 one company barracks was finished, a second was erected but not finished inside, the hospital was nearly completed except for some interior plastering, and a commissary storehouse and grain house were completed. Post Quartermaster George A. Hesselberger oversaw construction. Labor provided by the soldiers was joined by a large contingent of civilian workers. In September 1867, for example, there were 265 civilian employees (including 34 masons, 17 carpenters, 102 laborers, and 97 teamsters).

This set of officers' quarters, located just east of the commanding officer's quarters (stone structure at left) was home for Lieutenant John George Leefe's family, 1878–1880, when he served as post quartermaster.

The quartermaster reported the same month that 37 wagons and 224 mules were utilized in construction, "hauling Stone, Sand, lumber &c for the buildings now in course of erection." The civilian payroll for the month was $12,835.

During December 1867 and January 1868 the civilian employees were discharged for the winter by order of the department commander. The soldiers finished plastering the interior of the hospital, but no other work on new buildings was done until May 1868. During that month civilian employees again were hired to complete the commanding officer's quarters, several sets of officers' quarters, another company barracks, stables, and other necessary buildings. Some were built of stone and others of adobe bricks. Other buildings at the post included the post trader's store and saloon, built by the owner sometime after 1866 to replace the sod building that served as the first store.

When construction was completed, including several buildings erected after 1868, there were three barracks for enlisted men, two of stone and one of adobe, each 130 by 30 feet. The dormitory in each barracks contained twenty-two double two-tier bunks, providing sleeping space for eighty-eight men. Each bunk held four soldiers, two up and two down, who slept in opposite directions, head to toe. Opposing doors and windows provided ventilation, and the quarters were heated in the winter by wood-burning stoves. A water well was behind each barracks. A wooden shed was attached to the kitchens and contained a trough where the men could wash. The latrines were about thirty yards behind the quarters.

The commanding officer's quarters on the north side of the parade ground comprised a one-and-a-half-story stone building, fifty-two by thirty feet. It contained a central hall on the main floor, with two rooms on each side, eighteen feet square, and a kitchen twenty-six by sixteen feet attached to the rear of one side, forming an "L." Four attic rooms were on the upper floor. The lower rooms were heated by fireplaces. A frame stable and coach house was located north of the house.

Four sets of captain's quarters were housed in two duplexes, one of adobe covered with weather boarding and the other of frame with weather boarding, each forty-four by forty feet, and one and one-half stories high. Each set included a dining room, parlor, bedroom, kitchen, and three attic rooms. Six sets of lieutenant's quarters were located in three frame duplexes, each thirty-five by thirty-two feet, one and one-half stories high. Each set contained a dining room, bedroom, parlor, kitchen, and two attic rooms.

The laundresses and married soldiers were housed in the old dugouts and sod buildings along the river until new laundresses' quarters were constructed in 1875. The new quarters comprised eight sets in four duplexes, covered with boards set upright and battened, each thirty-two by sixteen feet. Each contained two rooms for a married soldier and his family. During the latter years, one of these quarters was used as the post school and reading room.

The commissary sergeant's quarters, thirty-two by fourteen feet, was constructed of boards set upright and battened. This building had three rooms and a kitchen. Another building, thirty-two by sixteen feet, frame construction, contained two sets of quarters, each with two rooms and a kitchen, for civilian employees. A similar structure, eighty by eighteen feet, provided three sets of quarters, each with one room and a kitchen, for civilian workers.

Two stone storehouses, each 130 by 30 feet, were located west of the parade. One served the quartermaster and the other the commissary, which had a cellar beneath for the storage of perishable items. Each building had two rooms partitioned off at the north end for offices. Between the two storehouses was a frame structure, 110 by 27 feet, used as a forage shed. Other buildings included a granary, twenty-eight by twelve feet; a coal shed, seventy-six by forty-one feet; a butcher shop, twenty-eight by seventeen feet; and the commanding officer's office and adjutant's office, thirty by twenty-five feet.

The quartermaster shops for the blacksmith, carpenter, and wheelwright were in a board and battened structure, ninety by twenty-five feet. The blacksmith shop contained three forges. A board and battened building, thirty-five by twenty-two feet, served as the paint shop. A board and battened lumber storehouse was forty-eight by twenty feet. Two buildings, each board and battened, sixteen by fourteen feet, served as the saddler's shop and as quarters for teamsters.

The first post bakery was built in the river bank in 1865. It was unsatisfactory, as Post Commander George A. Gordon explained in June 1866: "My present oven is dug in the side of the River bank and a great deal of the bread becomes Spoiled from dirt falling in the Dough During the process of baking." He requested three field ovens to use for the garrison until a better oven could be constructed. A new bake oven was

View of Fort Dodge from northwest with Arkansas River in background. The back side of the commanding officer's quarters is evident (tallest building near left), the rear of the post hospital is just right of center, and the post guardhouse is at far right. Although it is difficult to distinguish, an enlisted men's barracks may be seen through the gap between buildings just left of center (this gap is at the northwest corner of the parade ground). The post appeared more like a compact village than the popular image of an army fort.

27

View of Fort Dodge from the northeast, showing rear of commanding officer's quarters (large stone building left of center), flanked by a set of officers' quarters on either side, and the post hospital at right. The board fences were erected to keep livestock out of the post and enclose the backyards of the officers' quarters. Outhouses and storage sheds were located behind each set of officers' quarters, and the commanding officer's stable and carriage house was behind the commanding officer's quarters (building just right of center). The small structure outside the compound may have been a well house.

erected of stone, date unknown. It contained two large ovens with a capacity for baking five hundred rations of bread each day.

The stone hospital, ninety-seven by forty feet, was located at the northwest corner of the parade ground. The ward contained twelve beds. It was heated by wood-burning stoves and lighted by candles and oil lamps. A frame building, seventy-six by twenty-four feet, located about seventy-five feet west of the hospital served as a ward for black soldiers, with five beds and a hospital storeroom. In later years, when no black troops were present, this building provided quarters for hospital stewards and matrons. Other buildings included a hospital storehouse, forty by twenty-six feet, and a dead house, twelve by ten feet.

The guardhouse, described by the post surgeons as "a temporary wooden shed, 18 by 24 feet, in very bad condition and poorly adapted to the purposes for which it is used," was located west of the parade ground between the hospital and the storehouses. Another description of the guardhouse in 1875 revealed that the average occupancy of the building was twelve prisoners. Concerning living conditions therein, the surgeon wrote:

GROUND PLAN FORT DODGE.

ADJUTANT GENERALS LIBRARY

KANSAS

ESTABLISHED 1864

Latitude, 37° 44' 15" N. Longitude 99° 56' W.

MATERIALS OF BUILDINGS

STONE, CONSTRUCTED IN 1867

☐ ADOBE,   1868

△ WOOD   1870-77

FOR DIMENSIONS and COSTS of CONSTRUCTION
(WHERE KNOWN)
SEE OUTLINES OF BUILDINGS

Variation 15° East

FIELD TRAIN CORRAL, QMD
200 × 220
$1,59429/160

SHED

POST TRAIN CORRAL, QMD
68 × 220

CAVALRY CORRAL
68 × 220

TEAMSTERS QRTS   SADLER   TEAMSTERS QRS   CORRAL MASTER
16 × 30   16 × 28   16 × 18   16 × 20   14 × 16

TRADER STORE

POST SCHOOL

LAUNDRESSES
$78/.47 $78/.47
16 × 32   16 × 32

LAUNDRESSES
$78/.47 $78/.47
16 × 32   16 × 32

LIBRARY
14 × 20

WASH-HOUSE
16 × 24
24 × 52

WASH-HOUSE
16 × 24
24 × 52

WASH-HOUSE
16 × 24
24 × 52

BARRACKS
30 × 130

BARRACKS
30 × 130

BARRACKS
30 × 130

C. O.
STABLE
18 × 24

QUARTERS
24 × 40

COMDG OFFICER
16 × 22   30 × 52

OFFICERS
24 × 40

OFFICERS QUARTERS
22'-6"   22'-6"   22'-6"
32 ×   32 ×   32 ×

ICE HOUSE
30 × 35

DEAD HOUSE
10 × 12
$38.50

STORE ROOM
16 × 40
$450

HOSPITAL
30 × 67

30 × 40

10 × 18

DETACHED WARD
24 × 76

MAGAZINE
18 × 18
$973.47

GUARD HOUSE
26 × 90

Audr's office
20
82

SUBS Q.M.
31 × 130
25 × 106
31 × 130

WARE HOUSE

GRANARY
30 × 110
$1281 41

BAKE HOUSE
24 × 56

BUTCHER SHOP
17 × 28

COMMS'Y SERGT'S QRS.
33 × 14

ORD SERGT'S QRS.
32 × 14

BLACKSMITH'S & W. SHOPS
90 × 25 $732 87

CARPENTER SHOP
30 × 32

OLD B.S. SHOP

ARKANSAS RIVER

It is badly adapted for the purposes and impossible to keep it in good condition: repeated representations have been made of the necessity for a new guardhouse. Hitherto without effect. As there is no convenient latrine, during the night the prisoners are obliged to use a bucket for necessary purposes. At one time during the past year quite an epidemic of diarrhea occurred amongst the prisoners and with the convenience (or rather want of it) above referred to, the conditions of these unfortunates was deplorable; certainly not conducive to health or morals.

A new guardhouse was constructed a short time later. It was a frame building, thirty-six by fifty feet, with a secure room for prisoners and facilities for the guards.

A quartermaster corral was built with a sod wall along the north side and a shed extending the entire length of that wall on the inner side. The other sides of the corral were post and rail fence. In the corral's northeast corner were a forage room and harness room. The cavalry corral was completely enclosed with a sod wall and had a shed roof on three of the four sides. In 1873 a new cavalry stable was built, a frame structure with shingle roof measuring 168 by 240 feet.

After the railroad arrived and Dodge City was founded, the town became a major shipping point for cattle driven up the trails from Texas, 1876–1884. The herds of Texas longhorns generally were grazed on the grassland around Dodge City prior to shipment to the East. Many of the cattle came onto the military reservation and sometimes into the post proper. To keep the livestock out, a board fence was erected around the perimeter of the buildings in the late 1870s.

When construction was completed at the post Fort Dodge had a fine complement of sound and comfortable buildings. Some of those buildings are still in use as part of the Kansas Soldiers' Home, where they may be viewed to provide a better understanding of how the post buildings appeared.

The drinking water for the post was obtained from wells and reported by the post surgeons to be of excellent quality, and water for washing and extinguishing fires came from the river. Ice was cut from the frozen river during the winter months and stored in ice houses. On October 29, 1878, one of the two ice houses at Fort Dodge was destroyed by a fire started by a civilian employee's child who was playing with matches. The other ice house was not sufficient for the garrison. A frame coal house at abandoned Fort Larned was razed, and the lumber was used to erect another ice house at Fort Dodge.

Drainage of the post was accomplished by a trench from each of the quarters discharging into a larger drain that emptied into the river. The

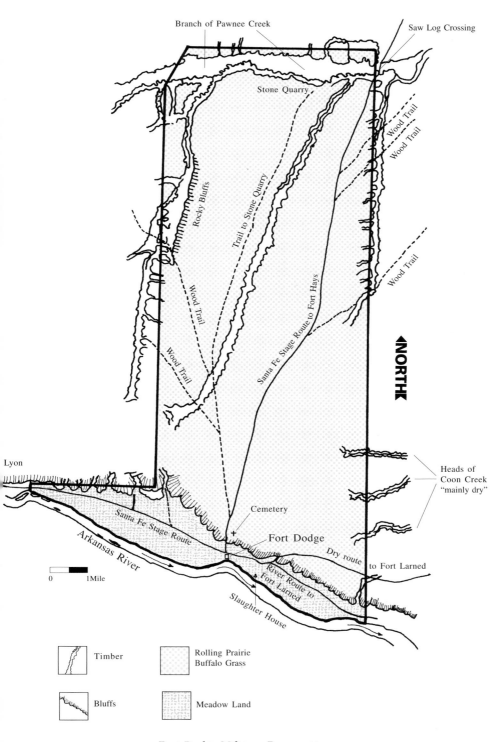

Branch of Pawnee Creek

Saw Log Crossing

Stone Quarry

Wood Trail

Wood Trail

Rocky Bluffs

Trail to Stone Quarry

Wood Trail

Santa Fe Stage Route to Fort Hays

Wood Trail

Wood Trail

◀NORTH

Lyon

Heads of
Coon Creek
"mainly dry"

Cemetery

Santa Fe Stage Route

+

Fort Dodge

Arkansas River

Dry route

to Fort Larned

0   1 Mile

River Route to
Fort Larned

Slaughter House

Timber		Rolling Prairie
Buffalo Grass
Bluffs		Meadow Land

Fort Dodge Military Reservation

garbage was dumped into the river below the post and carried off by the current. The post cemetery was located on top of the bluffs north of the post.

To protect the area immediately surrounding a military post from being settled under the several land laws of the United States, the practice had developed of establishing a military reservation. This prevented civilians from using up resources such as water, grass, stone, and timber that might be required by the post. The Fort Dodge Military Reservation was established on June 22, 1868.

The boot-shaped reserve included a tract that ran several miles along the north bank of the Arkansas River and extended northward some fourteen miles to include Sawlog Creek where timber and firewood could be obtained. The western toe of the boot was located on the one hundredth meridian, and the reserve was nearly seven miles across, east and west, at the widest point. The reservation, containing nearly sixty-eight square miles (43,461 acres), included the southern end of the Fort Hays–Fort Dodge Trail and later several miles of the Atchison, Topeka and Santa Fe Railroad. The town of Dodge City was laid out at the western tip of the boot in 1872. A portion of the reservation was located on Osage Trust Lands, for which that tribe was to be compensated when the lands were sold to private buyers.

By 1880 citizens were attempting to settle on the reserve and had to be removed by troops. In December 1880 Congress reduced the military reservation at Fort Dodge from the original 43,461 acres to 14,661 acres. All land north of the Atchison, Topeka and Santa Fe Railroad was opened to settlement, that portion of the reserve no longer being required by the army.

The railroad was permitted to purchase up to 160 acres adjoining the right-of-way and bought 142.15 acres at five dollars per acre. The remainder of the reservation north of the railroad was opened for homesteads and timber-culture claims as soon as the survey was completed. The remaining 14, 661 acres served as the military reservation until after the post was abandoned in 1882. By that time the garrison had fulfilled its military missions.

4

Mission Defined: Resolve the "Indian Problem" on the Plains

Fort Dodge, as noted, was part of a network of posts designed to bring peace to the Plains and resolve the "Indian problem." Thus the troops at Fort Dodge were assigned myriad tasks, the most important being to protect commerce and travel on the Santa Fe Trail, guard the mails and stagecoaches, and protect stage stations and settlements. They helped enforce treaties made with Indians when the government sought a peaceful solution, and they made war when the government decided that force was necessary to solve the problem.

Soldiers escorted stagecoaches and wagon trains during times of serious threats, scouted the region to watch for the location of Indian camps and signs of Indian troubles, and investigated reports of Indian hostilities. When depredations occurred, troops were sent to seek and punish the perpetrators and, if possible, recover property and people captured by Indians. They also participated in campaigns against hostile Indians, and Fort Dodge served as a base of operations or supply for some military expeditions. Soldiers stationed at the post helped safeguard the construction of the railroad when it reached the area, and protected the new settlements spawned by the railroads. While fulfilling these missions, the soldiers also had to build and maintain the post and perform all routine garrison duties.

During much of 1865, after the post was established in April, the troops spent more time constructing quarters than dealing with Indians.

This was not what military leaders had planned, but restrictions were placed on the army by civil authorities. General Dodge planned a major campaign against the Indians south of the Arkansas River in the spring of 1865, using Fort Dodge as one base of supplies for the troops in the field, but the expedition was canceled soon after it began.

A combination of factors, including public reaction to the Sand Creek Massacre and the conclusion of the Civil War, led to the ascendancy of the peace faction in the federal government. Congress created a new peace commission to negotiate with Plains Indians, and the army was directed to confine its operations north of the Arkansas River until the commission met with the Indians. The treaties of the Little Arkansas, previously noted, were signed in October 1865.

Thus the major military task for the soldiers at Fort Dodge during that first summer was to help keep the Indians south of the Arkansas River in order to protect traffic on the Santa Fe Trail from attack. This involved scouting along the trail in both directions and trying to prevent any Indians located from coming or staying north of the Arkansas. The troops were under strict orders not to cross the river and pursue Indians south of it.

During the spring and summer months, before the peace conference at the mouth of the Little Arkansas River (present Wichita, Kansas), Indians continued to raid in western Kansas. On June 8 a small party of Indians stole all the stock at Fort Dodge by disguising themselves in blue army coats and deceiving the herders until it was too late. Some of the stock was recovered. On June 12 Indians again raided the post and ran off some of the stock. Two employees at the sutler's store, Albert Weichselbaum and John Phennister, were killed. The next day everybody at the post worked to construct breastworks in case of another attack.

Raids along the Santa Fe Trail continued. In September a party of Kiowas attacked a Mexican wagon train near Fort Dodge and killed five men. The perpetrators were not found. They may have attended the peace conference a short time later and received annuities from the government for promising to keep the peace. Some of the Indians were ready to embrace peace, at least until the following spring.

The federal government had earlier signed treaties with most of the tribes on the Plains, offering food rations and other supplies each year in return for Indian promises not to molest U.S. citizens following the overland trails. The treaties of 1865 offered additional annuities in return for peace. Fort Dodge was designated as a distribution point for these annuities, from 1865 to 1869, for some members of five tribes—Comanches,

Edward Wanshear Wynkoop (left), 1836–1891, served as sheriff in western Kansas Territory (present Denver, Colorado) before the Civil War and was an officer in the First Colorado Infantry during the war. He commanded Fort Lyon, Colorado Territory, prior to the Sand Creek Massacre in November 1864 and later investigated that affair. Wynkoop commanded the escort for the commissioners at the Little Arkansas treaty negotiations in 1865, resigned from the service the following year to become agent for the Cheyenne, Arapaho, and Plains Apache tribes. His agency was at Fort Larned, but he also distributed annuities to the tribes at Fort Dodge. Wynkoop opposed General W.S. Hancock's treatment of Indians in 1867 and protested the burning of the village on Pawnee Fork. Likewise, he disapproved of the winter campaign, fearing it would punish peaceful Indians, and he resigned as agent at the time of the Battle of the Washita in 1868.

Kiowas, Plains Apaches, Cheyennes, and Arapahos. Thus the Indians came to the area to obtain their allotments, placing them in proximity to the trail and increasing the potential for trouble.

Although Indian troubles did not end with the Little Arkansas treaties, reports of depredations along the Santa Fe Trail virtually ceased for several months. An exception was a revenge attack on February 21, 1866 by four Cheyennes dressed in military coats and hats on the members of a wagon train belonging to Henderson Boggs and L. Meyer encamped on the north bank of the Arkansas River six miles below Fort Dodge. The Indians had appeared to be friendly and were given food and tobacco. Then, when riding away, they attacked the employees herding the livestock near the camp. They killed and scalped the sixteen-year-old son of Boggs and escaped with three stolen horses.

When Agent Edward Wanshear Wynkoop visited the Indians' camps to distribute supplies and encourage those who had not signed the Little Arkansas treaties to do so, he investigated this incident. The Indians admitted to the murder but claimed it was justified because Henderson Boggs had earlier been to the Cheyennes' camp to trade and had cheated one of the Indians. Captain Gordon, who commanded the escort that accompanied Wynkoop, explained: "On investigation it appears that Mr. Boggs went to the Indian camp without any authority whatever, and whilst there traded an Indian Eleven One Dollar Bills for Eleven Ten Dollar Bills. The Indian found him out, came over for revenge and unfortunately killed his son. I think this case needs no further comment."

The remainder of 1866 was the most peaceful in a decade, with only minor incidents noted. Some observers believed that lasting peace finally had been achieved, but those aware of the larger picture were not optimistic. Many members in each of the Plains tribes, most notably the Cheyenne Dog Soldiers, had not agreed to the 1865 treaties and refused to be bound by them. They were not willing to remain south of the Arkansas River. Also, the reservations had not been established and those Indians who had accepted the terms of the treaties continued to hunt between the Arkansas and the Platte.

Indians still roamed the lands through which the overland routes passed, and they gathered near the trail to receive their annuities. To some military leaders it seemed to be only a matter of time until some incident provoked hostilities. Precautions were taken but rarely needed because of the reduction in Indian activity. Indian Agent Wynkoop visited the Indian camps along the Arkansas valley in the spring of 1866 and declared they were all at peace. This remained the case along the Santa Fe Trail for the remainder of the year, but conflicts occurred along the trails farther north and in Texas.

The recovery of several members of the James Box family from the Kiowas and Kiowa Apaches in the autumn of 1866 was considered an important achievement in the chronicle of Fort Dodge. In August of that year Box, his wife, Mary, and their daughters Margaret (age seventeen), Josephine (age thirteen), Ida, and Laura were attacked by a party of Kiowas within three miles of their home in Montague County, Texas, just south of the Red River about midway between present Wichita Falls and Gainesville. The Kiowas did not consider the treaty agreements applicable to Texans and later argued they had not violated their promise not to raid Americans.

James Box was killed, scalped, and mutilated. His wife and daughters were taken captives. Mary Box later reported that they traveled on horseback for fourteen days to the Kiowas' village, during which time the baby, Laura, died. Sometime later Mary and Ida were traded to the Kiowa Apaches, and Margaret and Josephine were retained by the Kiowas. All reported they were required to perform drudge labor, and some were sexually abused.

On September 9 Kiowa Chief Satanta informed the commanding officer at Fort Larned, Major Cuvier Grover, that he held the Box family as captives and wished to return them. Major Grover notified Indian Agent I.C. Taylor at Fort Zarah. Taylor came to Fort Larned to secure the release of the prisoners only to discover that Satanta wanted a quantity of supplies in return. He informed Satanta that the treaty of the previous year required the return of all captives and also specified that nothing could be paid. He recommended that the Kiowas release the prisoners. Satanta requested time to think about it. Apparently it was at this point that Mrs. Box and Ida were traded to the Kiowa Apaches.

A short time later some scouts from Fort Dodge, who were circulating around the region in search of information about Indians, picked up the rumor that white women were being held captive in one of the Indian camps not far from the fort. Lieutenant George A. Hesselberger was sent with two privates and an interpreter, Fred Jones, to investigate.

At a Kiowa camp approximately thirty-five miles from the post Hesselberger and Jones were permitted to talk to Margaret and Josephine Box. The girls told about their capture and that their mother and sisters were with the Kiowa Apaches. Hesselberger tried to persuade the Kiowas to release the girls, but they refused. They would, however, trade the girls for guns, ammunition, coffee, sugar, and flour delivered to their camp.

The lieutenant returned to Fort Dodge and informed the commanding officer, Captain Andrew Sheridan, of the conditions. Sheridan resolved to ransom the young women and authorized the purchase of guns, powder, lead, knives, tobacco, coffee, sugar, flour, bread, rice, bacon, molasses, candles, matches, tin cups, shirts, cloth, blankets, hatchets, bugles, and some trinkets for the trade. These items were loaded into two wagons, and an ambulance was sent along to transport the girls. Lieutenant Hesselberger, Corporal Leander Herron, seven privates, and Fred Jones delivered the supplies.

Corporal Herron later claimed that Chief Satanta oversaw the exchange. Everything went as planned, and Margaret and Josephine were

General William Tecumseh Sherman, 1820–1891, earned a spectacular reputation during the Civil War and commanded the Military Division of the Missouri after the war. He supported construction of railroads in the West and was determined to remove Indian resistance throughout the region. Sherman inspected the military posts in his division, including Fort Dodge, and approved General Sheridan's plans for the winter campaign in 1868–1869. After Ulysses S. Grant became president, Sherman was promoted to general-in-chief of the army. He resigned that position in 1883 and retired in 1884.

brought safely to Fort Dodge. Herron also claimed that Margaret later gave birth to a child fathered by one of the Kiowas. It was hoped that Mary Box and the other girl would be traded when the parties holding them learned of the successful trade made by the Kiowas.

Meanwhile, however, the rules of the game were changed. General William T. Sherman, commander of the Military Division of the Missouri, visited Fort Dodge on October 6–8, 1866, just after the ransom had been accomplished. Sherman instructed Captain Sheridan not to send any more details on so hazardous a mission and not to trade any more goods for prisoners because it would encourage Indians to take more captives.

As expected, a few days later, a small party of Kiowa Apaches led by Chief Poor Bear came to Fort Dodge and offered to trade Mary Box and the other girl for supplies. Captain Sheridan was determined to recover the captives and decided to attempt a dangerous ruse that undoubtedly would not have been approved by his superiors. He had the interpreter inform the Indians that he was not allowed by his chief to send any more supplies to the Indians' camps, but if they would bring in the woman and her daughter, a council would be held to determine what could be done.

On October 19 a party of Kiowa Apaches set up camp about a mile down river from the fort. They sent word that they were ready to make a trade. Sheridan did not plan to trade anything for the captives. Instead he contrived to persuade several leaders to come into the post and hold them hostage until they surrendered the rest of the Box family.

Several of the Indians, suspecting nothing perverse, accepted the invitation and entered the post. They were prepared to bargain but discovered they were prisoners. They were directed to send one of their number to inform their compatriots of their situation and the terms for settlement. Within an hour Mrs. Box and Ida were turned over to the soldiers. Captain Sheridan had the interpreter inform the Indians that they were free to go but not to steal any more women and children.

General Sherman had authorized an issue of supplies from the post commissary to the Indians if the women were returned safely. The Kiowa Apaches were rewarded with 500 pounds of hard bread, 1,200 pounds of flour, 715 pounds of bacon, 354 pounds of roasted coffee, 1,451 pounds of sugar, 543 pounds of rice, 615 pounds of beans, 20 pounds of hominy, 4 gallons of molasses, 4 pounds of candles, 5 cans of jelly, and 6 cans of corn. The Indians may have considered that a fair trade.

The story of the Box family was utilized by the press to portray Indian atrocities and whip up public support for sending the army to strike first. The war department had been held in check since the Sand Creek Massacre, and the advocates of peace treaties and administration of tribal affairs by the Indian Bureau had been in ascendancy. Military leaders and public opinion in Kansas and across the Plains now claimed the peace efforts had failed and the war department should be placed in charge until the Indians were defeated. The railroad corporations wanted military protection and urged public officials to support the army.

During 1866 Indian hostilities increased in Texas where Kiowas and Comanches raided without restraint, on the Northern Plains where Red Cloud defeated troops along the Bozeman Trail, and along the Smoky Hill Trail where Cheyennes who rejected the treaties of the previous year began raiding. Military officials and civilians along the Santa Fe Trail feared that warfare might spread to include that overland route as well. Efforts by the Bureau of Indian Affairs to persuade the Indians who had signed the Little Arkansas treaties to accept amendments prohibiting them from hunting north of the Arkansas River and locating the reservations entirely outside the state of Kansas were not immediately successful. Attempts also failed to induce those tribesmen who had not signed the treaties to accept the terms.

39

Agent Wynkoop kept trying to win over the dissidents, but his efforts were frustrated by the aggressive attitude of the new commander of the Department of the Missouri, General Winfield Scott Hancock. He believed the army could resolve the problem with force and had little patience for peace treaties and the Indian Bureau. When Hancock learned that Cheyennes were raiding along the Smoky Hill Route, he threatened to send sufficient troops to punish them. Hancock did not trust the Indians and was prepared to believe the worst about them.

5

Mission Expanded: Hancock's War and the Medicine Lodge Treaties

Rumors had developed during the summer and fall of 1866 that the Indians were preparing to renew hostilities. General Sherman visited Fort Dodge in October on his tour of western Kansas and eastern Colorado Territory to investigate the situation. He saw little evidence of Indian hostility and reported as follows about the constant flow of unconfirmed reports that the tribes were preparing to fight: "These are all mysterious, and only accountable on the supposition that our people out West are resolved on trouble for the sake of the profit from military occupation."

The fears, real or imagined, led to additional requests for more military strength. General Sherman's suspicions were also confirmed. Some Kansas newspapers were accused of printing false reports of Indian attacks. Kansas Governor Samuel J. Crawford believed the Indians would not leave western Kansas until forced out by the army, and he urged an increase in troop strength at the forts. Some newspaper reporters, including Milton W. Reynolds of the Lawrence *Kansas State Journal*, accused Crawford and other officials of promulgating the fear of a general Indian uprising so they could raise a regiment of Kansas militia for federal service.

This idea was confirmed by Henry M. Stanley, correspondent for the St. Louis *Missouri Democrat*, and S. F. Hall, reporter for the *Chicago Tribune*. Hall wrote, "Governor Crawford does not breathe all peace but favors hostilities which will require enlistment of 10,000 Kansas troops." Crawford raised a battalion of Kansas volunteers in July 1867, the

General Winfield Scott Hancock, renowned for his Civil War record, commanded the Department of the Missouri in 1867. Anticipating a major Indian uprising on the Plains, Hancock led a strong force to western Kansas. The result was an increase in hostilities known as "Hancock's War." He was replaced later the same year by General Philip H. Sheridan after failing to bring peace to the Plains. Hancock ran for president in 1880 and was defeated by James A. Garfield.

Eighteenth Kansas Volunteer Cavalry, comprising four companies commanded by Major Horace L. Moore, and in 1868 he resigned as governor to organize and lead a regiment of Kansas volunteers against the Indians.

General Sherman's charge that war was promoted by those who would profit from it also was supported by facts. Those who supplied the army, carried freight to frontier posts, and transported supplies and equipment into the field for military expeditions, could reap fortunes if fighting continued. The railroads, as noted, wanted Indian threats removed. Governor Crawford was later charged with accepting a bribe from one of the railroads. An investigation exonerated him, but he did receive 640 acres of land from the company. Thus rumors of war may have had as much to do with politics and economics as with the disposition of the Plains tribes.

During the winter of 1866–1867 more rumors spread that a major uprising would come the following spring, destroying the peace of the previous year. Interpreter Fred Jones picked up rumors of Indian plans to unite and strike hard in 1867. In January 1867 he persuaded post commander Major Henry Douglas, Third Infantry, that the rumors were true and the Indians were accumulating large supplies of carbines, revolvers, powder, and lead from the traders licensed by the Bureau of Indian Affairs.

Henry Stanley implicated Charley Rath, an Indian trader who later became a Dodge City merchant, as one who sold arms and whiskey to the

Henry M. Stanley, newspaper reporter, accompanied the Hancock Expedition in 1867 and attended the Medicine Lodge Treaty council later that year. When he arrived at Fort Dodge with Hancock in April 1867 he wrote, "the fort is kept as neat as possible." Stanley later became famous for finding David Livingstone in Africa in 1871. This sketch appeared in Harper's Weekly, *July 27, 1872.*

Indians. Major Douglas declared that Rath "has armed several bands of Kiowas with Revolvers and has completely overstocked them with Powder." It was illegal to trade alcohol to Indians, and evidence supports that whiskey was a factor in Indian–white conflicts on the Plains. Indians who rejected the treaties, were well supplied with arms and ammunition, and had access to whiskey were truly a potential threat to travelers and settlers.

Douglas was alarmed and conveyed his fears to General Hancock, who was predisposed to believe the Indians were preparing for war. In an attempt to control the sale of arms, Hancock directed that no weapons or ammunition be traded to Indians by anyone except authorized traders and only at Forts Larned and Dodge. The post commanders were to permit the sale of ammunition to Indians only in such quantities as they considered necessary for hunting.

In February 1867 Major Douglas communicated additional disquieting information to General Hancock. He had met with Kiowa Chief Satanta who said he did not want war but wanted the whites to leave the region. He warned that the whites must stop killing buffalo and cutting wood. The following month Arapaho Chief Little Raven made a similar request and asked the army to leave Fort Dodge before the grass was green. Also, Fred Jones reported that Chief Satanta had directed him to carry a message to the commander of Fort Dodge. The Kiowa chief demanded that all military posts be closed, the soldiers withdrawn, traffic on the Santa Fe Trail stopped at Council Grove, and the railroad halted at Junction City. If this were not done, Satanta threatened to join with the other tribes, drive out the soldiers, and close the wagon road.

According to Jones, Satanta made one more audacious declaration. He said his livestock was getting weak and tired, and he wanted the government stock better fed because he would come to Fort Dodge to take the animals before the soldiers left. Major Douglas, anticipating a raid, established a plan of action at the post. It was later determined that Jones had fabricated some of this report and misrepresented Satanta's request, but Major Douglas never communicated that to General Hancock. Hancock had received similar reports from Captain Henry Asbury at Fort Larned.

The first recorded difficulty with Indians occurred on March 10, 1867, when eight Cheyennes ran off forty mules from a wagon train encamped about 120 miles west of Fort Dodge. The same party stole four mules and two horses from a party of trappers on the upper Cimarron River. The trappers retaliated a few weeks later and stole twelve horses from an Arapaho camp under the leadership of Chief Little Raven, an advocate of peace with the whites. Such incidents threatened the tenuous peace.

After hearing the rumors of anticipated hostilities, and before hearing of these raids, Hancock was convinced that a major Indian uprising could be expected in the spring of 1867. He never investigated the stories nor visited the posts in western Kansas. Instead, after obtaining approval from General Sherman, he began to organize a large military force to march across the Plains to intimidate the Indians. He instructed the Indian agents to notify their tribes that a big army was coming "to show the Indians within the limits of this department that we are able to chastise any tribes who may molest people who are travelling across the plains. It is not our desire to bring on difficulties with the Indians, but to treat them with justice and according to our treaty stipulations."

Hancock organized the expedition at Fort Riley, amassing fourteen hundred troops comprised of a battery of Fourth Artillery, seven companies of Thirty-seventh Infantry, eleven troops of Seventh Cavalry, and a squadron of the Corps of Engineers. Scouts for the campaign included James B. (Wild Bill) Hickok, Jack Harvey, Tom Atkins, Edmund Guerrier, and fifteen Delaware Indians under Fall Leaf. The expedition was accompanied by a large supply train.

The troops left Fort Riley on March 26, 1867, and marched to Forts Harker, Zarah, and Larned, arriving there April 7. At least forty soldiers deserted during the trip. Relying on Indian Agents Wynkoop and Jesse Leavenworth to arrange conferences with representatives of the various

This sketch of the captured Cheyenne lodges on Pawnee Fork appeared in Harper's Weekly, *May 11, 1867.*

tribes, Hancock looked forward to a council with Cheyennes and Brulé Sioux at Fort Larned on April 10. Approximately fifteen hundred of those people were encamped on Pawnee Fork about thirty-five miles from the post.

A spring snowstorm on April 9 blanketed the area with eight inches of snow, delaying the meeting. On April 12 two Cheyenne chiefs, Tall Bull and White Horse, both Dog Soldiers, and several warriors came to meet Hancock. The general was disappointed to see so few Indians and told them he would march his troops to their camp the next day. Tall Bull discouraged this, perhaps fearing an attack on the village.

Hancock was determined to proceed, and the next day his troops marched twenty-one miles and went into camp beside Pawnee Fork. The Indians set fire to the grass below their village, which irritated Hancock who believed the Indians either had something to hide or, worse, planned to escape. The soldiers crossed the stream and pushed on toward the village.

Soon they were met by Brulé Sioux Chief Pawnee Killer, Cheyenne Chief White Horse, and a few others. Pawnee Killer and White Horse requested that Hancock not march his troops to their village because it would frighten the women and children. The two Indians agreed to remain in Hancock's camp during the night and have other leaders come the next day for the council.

The next morning, April 14, Pawnee Killer left camp to locate the other chiefs. Hancock expected them at 9:00 A.M. When they had not arrived at 11:00 A.M., Hancock moved his troops toward the village. After traveling a few miles they encountered several hundred Indians blocking their path. Hancock formed his soldiers into a line of battle. Agent Wynkoop intervened and learned the reason for the Indians' delay: their camp was farther away than Hancock had supposed. A conference was quickly arranged between the two lines.

Hancock and members of his staff met with about a dozen Indian leaders. The Indians stated they were for peace but wanted the soldiers to stay away from their village. Hancock said he would move the troops and encamp near the Indians, promising to keep the soldiers from entering the Indian village, and they would negotiate the following day. That afternoon the troops camped on the North Fork of the Pawnee about a half mile from the three hundred Cheyenne and Sioux lodges. Several Cheyennes explained to Hancock that the women and children had fled from the village when the troops approached because they feared an attack similar to that at Sand Creek. The surgeon with the expedition, Isaac Coates, recorded that "the women and children were so terrified on seeing the troops approach" that they "ran off leaving everything behind them."

Hancock assured them they were safe and asked them to bring the people back to their village. They did not come, and by sunset scouts reported that the remainder of the Indians were preparing to leave too. Hancock sent Lieutenant Colonel (Brevet Major General) George A. Custer with a detachment of Seventh Cavalry to surround the Indian camp and prevent the Indians' flight. Custer was too late, for the entire village had escaped. Only an elderly Sioux man, an aged Indian woman, and one sickly Indian girl remained. These "captives" were later taken to Fort Dodge.

The elderly Sioux man died of "old age" at the post on June 23, 1867. The Indian woman, tribe not identified, escaped on July 1 and was not found. The Indian girl died at Fort Dodge on July 24. The cause of death was not given.

At Pawnee Fork, Hancock concluded that the Indians must be guilty of hostile actions or they would not have fled. He reported, "This looks like the commencement of war." Surgeon Coates noted a change in purpose of the expedition: "Up to this time, the mission of the troops on the Plains had been to scare the Indians, henceforth, to war upon them." Custer and the cavalry were sent in pursuit but failed to overtake the fleeing Indians. Custer reached the Smoky Hill Trail on April 17, where he learned that some of the stage stations had been attacked by unidentified Indians. He immediately sent a courier to report to Hancock, still holding the abandoned Indian camp.

Old Sioux Indian Captured by General Hancock *from Harper's Weekly, May 11, 1867. This elderly man remained in the abandoned village and may have been sick. He was taken to Fort Dodge where he was kept as a prisoner until his death of "old age" two months later.*

Custer went to Fort Hays, where he remained for a month awaiting supplies. He later pursued the Indians for several weeks without success.

After hearing from Custer, Hancock ordered that the captured village be destroyed. Agent Wynkoop protested, but the tipis and supplies were burned on April 19, as Hancock proclaimed, "as a punishment for the bad faith practiced by the Cheyenne and Sioux." The destruction of the village precipitated an increase in Indian hostilities. Hancock's prediction of an uprising in the spring of 1867 was fulfilled, although he may have been a significant contributing factor.

Hancock marched the remainder of his command to Fort Dodge where, according to Henry Stanley, he "was greeted by a salute of fifteen guns, and the garrison at the same time was turned out, and presented arms." There Hancock hoped to meet with representatives of the Kiowas, Arapahos, and Comanches. Arriving at the post on April 22, Hancock was informed that Major Wickliffe Cooper, Seventh Cavalry, with a detachment of 130 men of his regiment, had encountered a small party of Cheyennes near Cimarron Crossing a few days earlier.

Cooper had directed his subordinate, Lieutenant Matthew Berry, and twenty men to demand the warriors' surrender. The Indians resisted and,

This sketch by Theodore Davis, showing the burning of the Cheyenne and Sioux village on Pawnee Fork, April 19, 1867, appeared in Harper's Weekly, June 8, 1867.

in the brief engagement, six Cheyennes were killed, one trooper was wounded, and one horse was shot. The scalp of a white woman was found among the effects of one of the dead Indians. Agent Wynkoop again protested, declaring that the six Cheyennes had done nothing to provoke the attack. Lieutenant Berry was instructed "that friendly Indians must not be molested." Even so, the skirmish was another sign of developing conflict that soon spread across the region.

On April 23 Hancock met with Kiowa chiefs Kicking Bird and Stumbling Bear and several of their tribesmen. They declared the Kiowas wanted peace. Hancock offered to enlist members of the tribe as scouts for the army. Kicking Bird said he would have to confer with other chiefs, including Satanta, Satank, Heap of Bears, Lone Wolf, Black Bird, and Little Heart, before making his decision.

Kicking Bird informed Hancock that the Arapahos had been at Fort Dodge to see him but had tired of waiting and gone south. Kicking Bird offered to find the Arapahos and send them back if Hancock desired. The general wanted to meet as many Indians as possible and accepted the offer.

While waiting, Hancock arranged for better protection of the Santa Fe Trail, assigning one company of Thirty-seventh Infantry from his expedition to Forts Dodge, Larned, and Lyon. These troops were directed to provide escorts for stagecoaches. In addition, Hancock detailed one company of Seventh Cavalry to Fort Dodge and one to Fort Lyon to help patrol the roads and scout for hostile bands of Indians. To centralize command of these forces, Hancock appointed Major Henry Douglas, commander at Fort

General Hancock met with Kiowa chiefs at Fort Dodge in April 1867, and these sketches of three chiefs, identified as Atalie, Stumbling Bear, and Kicking Bird, appeared in Harper's Weekly, May 25, 1867.

Dodge, to oversee protection of the Southern Overland Mail route between Forts Zarah and Lyon. Douglas stationed one noncommissioned officer and nine privates at each stage station. Each stagecoach was escorted by ten soldiers transported in six-mule army wagons. The remainder of the Seventh Cavalry, under Custer's command, were to continue to search for warlike Indians along the Smoky Hill and Platte River roads.

Hancock was especially pleased with Fort Dodge and commended Major Douglas for a job well done. He encouraged the rapid completion of the buildings there and noted that when completed Fort Dodge would be the "most desirable post" in western Kansas. He declared that the troops were well disciplined and the post was the only one in the department fully capable of defending itself.

Hancock had originally planned to travel south from Fort Dodge to try to visit Kiowa and Comanche camps. However, because Custer was detained on the Smoky Hill and a portion of the command had been sent to posts along the Santa Fe Trail, Hancock now considered his expedition too small to intimidate the Indians. Therefore, he returned to Fort Larned to meet with Kiowas and Comanches that Agent Leavenworth could induce to come there.

On April 28 Arapaho Chief Little Raven and several of his warriors arrived at Fort Dodge. Little Raven pledged to abide by the terms of the Little Arkansas treaties and denied that his people had participated in

Indian Council at Fort Dodge, Kansas, between General Hancock and the Kiowa Chiefs, *sketched by Theodore R. Davis, from* Harper's Weekly, *May 25, 1867.*

any raids against Americans. He promised to stay south of the Arkansas River and not cause any trouble along the Santa Fe Trail. Hancock also secured a pledge from the chief not to raid in Texas.

General Hancock, pleased with Little Raven's promises, left Fort Dodge the same day to go to Fort Larned. Along the way, at Big Coon Creek, he met Kiowa Chief Satanta. Because Satanta wanted to talk with Hancock, the general asked Satanta to accompany him to Fort Larned. They reached the post early afternoon on April 30.

On May 1 Hancock and Satanta met, with Fred Jones as interpreter. Although it had been reports of Satanta's demands for the removal of all whites from the region that had helped persuade Hancock to launch his expedition, Satanta proclaimed he and his people wanted peace and would not attack Americans. He declared he had worked hard to persuade the Kiowas to be peaceful, and they would not molest travelers on the Santa Fe Trail. He did express opposition to the railroad. He also accused Agent Leavenworth of withholding the Kiowas' annuities and cheating them.

Leavenworth explained that Satanta had been involved in the capture of the Box family the previous year, and he had been instructed to withhold annuities until all captives had been returned and the Kiowas promised not to raid. Hancock reminded the chief of his raids in Texas, chided him for threatening troops at forts along the Santa Fe Trail, and explained that in the Little Arkansas Treaty he had consented to the building of the railroad.

Satanta declared he and his people would keep the peace, would even fight other Indians to protect the whites if necessary. Hancock offered to enlist Kiowas to serve as scouts for the army, but Satanta declined.

Hancock seemed satisfied by the peaceful declarations of the Indians he had met, unable to differentiate between hostile and peaceful Indians even in council. In fact, Hancock was so impressed with Satanta, who had a reputation as an orator, that he presented him a major general's dress coat, sash, and plumed hat. Satanta was proud of the gift and later wore it to taunt soldiers while breaking the peace, which included stealing a horse herd at Fort Dodge a few weeks later.

Hancock was disappointed that no other Kiowa or Comanche leaders met him at Fort Larned, and he headed for Fort Hays on May 2. After visiting other posts and making a trip to Denver, Hancock returned to Fort Leavenworth. Agent Leavenworth was critical of Hancock's efforts, declaring, "I am sorry to say that, in my opinion, little good, but a great deal of harm, has resulted from this expedition." Surgeon Coates concluded that General Hancock "had been sent out to do what could not be done. . . . The only criticism that can be justly made against the General is that he did not exercise that good common sense and military discretion in this expedition, which characterized him during the Rebellion." Henry M. Stanley declared that "Hancock obeyed his orders to the very letter." Even so, the conflicts of 1867 were dubbed "Hancock's War."

The troops at Fort Dodge were involved in the strife, and Indian raids occurred near and at the post. On June 5 Indians believed to be Kiowas attacked a Mexican wagon train south of the Arkansas near the mouth of Mulberry Creek and killed four teamsters, wounded several others, and stole ninety-six cattle, "several" horses and mules, and the contents of some of the wagons. The following day a Mexican wagon train located south of the Arkansas River near Cimarron Crossing was attacked and lost much of its livestock. A Mexican boy, known only as Ramon, received an arrow wound during the attack and died at the Fort Dodge hospital on June 15.

Major Douglas declared "the disaster to the trains was owing to the gross carelessness of the men in charge." The men with the train near Mulberry Creek had left their arms in the wagons at the time of the attack. Douglas sent all available troops from the post to provide relief for the victims and search for the raiders. They failed to find the Indians.

51

A few days later, June 12, Chief Satanta and an estimated two hundred Kiowas made a surprise raid at Fort Dodge at about 8:00 A.M., attempting to capture the mules and horses grazing near the post under guards. The quartermaster mules were driven to the post as soon as the Indians were seen, but most of the cavalry horses were more than a mile east of the post and all were lost. One of the guards, Private James Spillman, Company B, Seventh Cavalry, was wounded and later died. It was reported that Satanta was wearing the officer's coat and hat given him earlier by General Hancock, and that he waved the plumed hat at the soldiers in the fort as the horse herd was driven away.

Ten horses had not been turned out to graze, and these were mounted by a small detachment that pursued the Kiowas. As soon as possible several wagons were hitched to mules and carried infantrymen in the chase. Several miles from the post they found a few Indians, including Satanta, trying to catch several horses that had strayed from the herd. They killed Satanta's horse, but the chief was unscathed, and the Indians escaped with the captured stock. Major Douglas informed General Hancock, "I shall consider myself at war with all Indians, until I receive instructions from you."

Indian attacks at stage stations on the Santa Fe Trail increased along with the assaults on wagon trains. The casualties mounted up, and the Indians became more brazen. Additional soldiers were sent to help guard the stage stations, but Major Douglas was unable to provide much relief to wagon trains because of the loss of the cavalry horses.

On June 18, 1867, Major Douglas requested permission to hire three additional civilian scouts to help find the Indians, noting that two days previous a party of Cheyennes and Sioux had attacked the stage station at Cimarron Crossing, killed two American citizens belonging to a wagon train crossing the river there, and stolen eight mules and twenty cattle. He declared, "The Country is swarming with Indians." He was frustrated that he could not retaliate effectively.

More Indian raids followed. On July 19 they attacked a government contract wagon train about fifteen miles west of Fort Dodge and killed a

Treaty council at Medicine Lodge Creek, October 1867. Sketch from Harper's Weekly, *November 16, 1867.*

boy and an ox. A large Mexican wagon train with 130 men under charge of José Guttierrez was set upon by an estimated sixty Indians south of Cimarron Crossing a short time later. This train lost two men killed and three wounded, and the Indians seized 530 cattle. The same day a small party of civilians cutting hay near Cimarron Crossing was attacked and lost two killed and one wounded. Major Douglas dispatched infantrymen to investigate and assist, but they found no Indians.

The soldiers' inability to catch and punish Indians elicited criticism from the public and the press. The editor of the *Junction City Union* wrote on June 29, 1867: "There does not appear to be enough soldiers to protect the Santa Fe Route, let alone hunt Indians. I can't tell what the devil the government means, men are being butchered every day and no attempt is made to bring the war to a close." The army did not have the manpower, and more important the Indians were able to avoid the soldiers almost at will. It was virtually impossible for soldiers, most of whom had little understanding of Indians, to capture or defeat the Indians in their own territory, particularly during the spring and summer seasons. A winter campaign might be a different story.

Much of "Hancock's War" was north of the Arkansas River and Fort Dodge, and involved Custer's command as well as troops stationed at Forts Hays and Wallace on the Smoky Hill Route. The hostile Indians were seldom found and certainly not subdued. Custer abandoned his troops at Fort Wallace and made a forced march to see his wife, Elizabeth, at Fort Riley. He was arrested, tried by court-martial, and suspended from rank and pay for one year. Offensive actions against the Indians were discontinued later in the summer. Hancock had improved the defense of the overland trails by increasing the number of troops assigned to garrison the posts and guard stage stations. He also inspected the forts and recommended improvements. He did not, however, find a solution to Indian resistance on the Plains.

By the late summer of 1867 Indians were wreaking havoc along the trails and among the settlements of western Kansas. Near Fort Dodge, on

September 6, a party cutting hay was attacked by Indians believed to be Arapahos, resulting in one citizen killed and a team of mules stolen. The same day interpreter Fred Jones and another man were attacked by Arapahos between Fort Dodge and Fort Larned. They managed to escape unharmed.

On September 10 Major Douglas, commanding Fort Dodge, reported that "a train loaded with stores for this post, Albino Ortega wagon master, was attacked by Indians while en route from Fort Harker on the river road, about 20 miles from this post; five wagons were cut off & plundered, one teamster killed & a considerable amount of Ammunition, Ordnance & Quartermaster Stores carried away." Early in October woodcutters John Felch and James Young, employed by the wood contractor at Fort Dodge, were killed and scalped about sixteen miles from the post. Similar raids were reported near other military posts.

The official report counted 128 whites killed in Kansas during 1867, more than in any previous year. If the army could not bring peace, perhaps treaty negotiations could end the war.

While the Hancock Expedition was still in the field advocates for a peaceful solution to the "Indian problem" were pushing for another council and more treaties. Congress created the Indian Peace Commission in July 1867. The conjecture was that war would not end as long as Indians occupied lands whites wanted. The solution proposed was the same as in 1865—place the Indians on reservations. The results were the Medicine Lodge treaties signed in October 1867 with some leaders of the Kiowas, Comanches, Plains Apaches, Cheyennes, and Arapahos.

The agreements provided that all hostilities would cease immediately, those who violated the peace in the future would be punished, and reservations would be established. The Indians surrendered all claims to lands between the Arkansas and Platte Rivers and agreed not to hunt in that region. They promised not to oppose the railroads. The government was to provide annuities, schools and teachers, hospitals and doctors, blacksmiths, agricultural implements, and seed.

Peace settled over the Plains for the winter months, but travelers and settlers feared that spring would see a renewal of hostilities. Some factions within the tribes refused to accept the treaties and were determined to fight to retain their claims to lands in Kansas as long as possible. The Indians who placed their mark on the agreements also returned to Kansas the following spring. The U.S. Senate did not approve the treaties until July 1868, and these were signed by the president the following month. Congress then had to appropriate funds to fulfill obligations to the Indians. But long before that happened the Indian war of 1868 began.

6

Mission Continued:
The War of 1868 and the
Winter Campaign

Kiowa Chief Satanta, who had returned to Fort Dodge in late February 1868, was involved in the first recorded incidence of violence that year. When his party returned to their reservation, the Kiowas attacked white hunters near Crooked Creek, reportedly killing one and taking all their property. Major Douglas knew that by terms of the recent treaty with the Kiowas, whites were not permitted south of the Arkansas River. Therefore, he stated, "I believe that Satanta considers it perfectly proper to attack the property of any parties there found." The February 1868 attack was a precursor of what was to come.

Early in the spring of 1868 many of the Plains Indians moved from their winter camps to the south and located near Forts Dodge and Larned, as they had been doing since the 1865 treaties, to draw government rations until the grass greened up and they could hunt buffalo. Some Kiowas, Plains Apaches, Comanches, and Southern Cheyennes camped near Fort Larned. A few Kiowas and Comanches, the remainder of Southern Cheyennes, and Southern Arapahos located near Fort Dodge. In April one band of Kiowas moved to Bluff Creek south of Fort Dodge and reported to the commanding officer at the post that Texans were "on the warpath after them." Most Kiowas, Plains Apaches, and Comanches remained in present Oklahoma and raided into Texas until early summer, when they also encamped along the Santa Fe Trail.

Satanta was the most colorful leader of the Kiowas, considered to be a great orator and defender of his people. He impressed General Hancock with his pledges of peace in 1867, but Satanta continued to oppose the increasing migration of Euro-Americans into Kiowa lands. He located on a reservation after the winter campaign of 1868–1869. Later he was arrested, along with Satank and Big Tree, tried, and convicted for the attack on the Warren wagon train in Texas. Satanta was confined in the Texas penitentiary. He died there in 1874, reportedly committing suicide. Although the army found Satanta to be a vocal and formidable enemy, he was recognized as an exceptional protector of his people and their traditional way of life. The town of Satanta in southwest Kansas was named to honor this Kiowa leader.

By April 1868 an estimated eighty-six hundred Indians were in the region of western Kansas and eastern Colorado. Agent Wynkoop reported that these Indians were hungry and in need of assistance. He believed that a liberal supply of food would keep them satisfied and prevent hostilities. He planned to distribute food at Fort Dodge and requisitioned seventy-four hundred rations per day to be delivered there. Congress had not yet appropriated funds for new annuities, however, and the supplies available were limited.

Without sufficient rations, some Indians began harassing wagon trains to obtain supplies. Commissioner of Indian Affairs Nathaniel G. Taylor explained that the Indian uprising of 1868 resulted from "the fact that the department, for want of appropriations, was compelled to stop their supplies, and to permit them to recur to the chase for subsistence." In addition, when conflicts occurred, the guns and ammunition promised the Indians were withheld. This further upset the tribesmen. They concluded the government was not honoring the Medicine Lodge treaties, and thus they were free to violate the agreements too.

General Philip H. Sheridan, who had replaced Hancock as commander of the Department of the Missouri, visited posts along the Santa Fe

Trail in the spring to assess the state of affairs. At Fort Dodge he found hundreds of encamped Indians, who sent a delegation to meet with Sheridan and discuss their situation. The general refused to meet them, stating that he had no authority to bargain with Indians. They would have to plead their case with the Indian Bureau through their agents. Sheridan later declared: "My refusal left them without hope of securing better terms, or of even delaying matters longer; so henceforth they were more than ever reckless and defiant."

Sheridan learned that the Indians were unhappy with the reservations assigned to them and did not plan to remove their permanently. They considered the treaty to be important only for their attainment of annuities. Since funds for additional annuities had not yet been provided, the Indians, according to Sheridan, were "insolent and overbearing." This caused him "to take all precautions in my power to protect . . . lines of travel." He appointed scouts to keep him informed of Indian activities, and he returned to Fort Leavenworth.

It was relatively quiet along the Arkansas River until June, except for the occasional harassment of a wagon train by Indians seeking coffee, sugar, and food. In June a party of Cheyennes attacked Kansa Indians near Council Grove, and the fighting spread as Cheyennes attacked white settlements along the Solomon River and other streams. In July, as previously noted, more Kiowas and Comanches arrived in Kansas to collect their annuities, which were not available. Hostilities increased.

Governor Samuel J. Crawford became irate at the inability of federal troops to protect Kansas citizens. On August 24 he appealed to President Andrew Johnson for relief:

> The Indians are again committing depredations in Western Kansas.
> Last week they killed and wounded thirty men, women and children, ravished seven women and carried away one young lady—burned a number of houses and captured a large amount of stock and other property.
> Frontier settlers were driven in some sixty miles, leaving everything at the mercy of these red-handed fiends.

Crawford offered to raise volunteers to help fight and begged that the Kiowas, Comanches, Arapahos, Plains Apaches, and Cheyennes "be driven, at once, from this state." He called the Peace Commission "a mockery and a disgrace to the nation." General Sheridan, without enough troops to control the situation, could do little more than take defensive actions during the summer months. He estimated the combined tribes had about six thousand warriors available, while his troops comprised

General Philip Henry Sheridan, 1831–1888, was a career officer who achieved fame as a cavalry commander during the Civil War. He replaced General Hancock as commander of the Department of the Missouri in February 1868. He developed plans to defeat hostile Indians of the Plains, his strategies including Forsyth's Scouts and the winter campaign of 1868–1869. In 1869 he succeeded General William Tecumseh Sherman as commander of the Military Division of the Missouri and directed military operations on the Plains until 1883, when he succeeded Sherman as general-in-chief of the army. He held that office until his death. Sheridan visited Fort Dodge several times and departed from there for the winter campaign in 1868.

approximately fourteen hundred infantry and twelve hundred cavalry. After distributing these soldiers at military posts and stage stations and providing protection for the railroad building along the Smoky Hill Trail, some eight hundred men were available for offensive duties. As this was inadequate for the task at hand, these men were divided and stationed at Fort Dodge and Walnut Creek Crossing on the Fort Hays–Fort Dodge Trail. This was the main route of military supplies from the railroad at Hays City to Fort Dodge, and from there to other posts south and west.

When Sheridan requested more troops, especially cavalry, General Sherman sent seven companies of the Fifth Cavalry from several southern states. These reinforcements were concentrated at Fort Harker from where they moved onto the Plains to seek and punish hostile Indians until the winter campaign began.

Before additional troops arrived to initiate a major campaign to find hostile tribesmen, Indian attacks on travelers and settlers became more frequent and deadly On August 12 a band of Cheyennes attacked and robbed the camp of Robert Wright, lime contractor for the post. The same day another band took 129 mules and 3 horses from a Mexican wagon train north of Cimarron Crossing. On August 17 or 18 a war party of Cheyennes ran off cattle from a ranch near Pawnee Fork. Troops under command of Lieutenant David W. Wallingford, Seventh Cavalry, were sent to recover the livestock but failed to find any Indians or cattle. On August 21 about one hundred lodges of Arapahos camped a mile west of Fort Dodge and reported that Cheyennes were making preparations to attack the fort. On August 25 Indians attacked the wood contractor's train hauling wood from Pawnee Fork and speared the wagon master.

On August 24, 1868, the same day Governor Crawford appealed to President Andrew Johnson for help, General Sheridan declared war against the Cheyennes and Arapahos for "the recent open acts of hostility . . . embracing the murder of twenty unarmed citizens of the State of Kansas, the wounding of many more, and acts of outrage against women and children, too atrocious to mention in detail." The Indians were to be forced onto the reservations and "compelled to deliver up the perpetrators of the guilty acts."

Kiowas, Plains Apaches, and Comanches were not included in the declaration because it was believed they had moved south of the Arkansas after receiving annuities early in August. Many of these passed by Fort Dodge. On August 6 and 7, for example, 973 men, women, and children of three tribes passed the post, moving south. It was soon discovered that they had moved the women and children south of the Arkansas, but some of the warriors had come back to raid along the Santa Fe Trail.

In an attempt to keep Kiowas, Plains Apaches, and Comanches from engaging in the Indian war, General William B. Hazen was sent to Fort Cobb, Indian Territory, to furnish provisions to all members of these tribes who came to their reservation. All Indians not on their reservations were considered to be hostile, and war would be made against them until they either accepted the reservations or were annihilated.

It was one thing to declare war and state its purposes; it was quite another to fulfill the goals. Sheridan planned to strike Indian villages, especially during the winter months when it would be more difficult for the Indians to flee and the destruction of their homes and supplies would be more crucial. If the army could destroy the Indians' ability to sustain their traditional way of life, they would be forced to become dependent on the government and stay on the reserves.

Lieutenant Colonel (Brevet Brigadier General) Alfred Sully, Third Infantry, was directed to begin offensive operations in September. He was expected to harass the Indians with a small force until more troops could be brought into the region. Sully arrived at Fort Dodge on September 1 to organize his command. Sheridan arrived the next day to oversee the prepara-

Little Raven, Arapaho chief, holding a girl believed to be his granddaughter, with William Bent and Little Raven's sons Archer and Manimick. The photo was taken at Fort Dodge in 1867 by Second Lieutenant Philip Reade, Third Infantry, who arrived at Fort Dodge in July 1867. The onlookers on the roof are not identified.

tions. Sully had nine companies of Seventh Cavalry commanded by Major Joel Elliott and three of Third Infantry commanded by Captain John Henry Page, in all nearly six hundred officers and men. John Smith, Ben Clark, and Amos Chapman were hired as guides. Supplies came by railroad to Fort Hays and by wagon train on to Fort Dodge. From there a supply train accompanied the expedition, returning to the post for replenishment as needed.

Sully was directed to move south of the Arkansas River and strike Indian villages reported to be along the Cimarron River. It was believed that, if he threatened the camps of Indian women and children, the warriors would come back from western Kansas to protect them. This would relieve pressure on the settlements and trails. Later, when reinforcements arrived, a winter campaign would attack the Indians in their camps.

As Sully was preparing to take the field, Indians continued to raid. On September 1 a Mexican came to Fort Dodge and told how he had escaped from a wagon train attacked by Indians near Cimarron Crossing. The men of the train had defended themselves for four days, and he had been sent to the fort for relief. Lieutenant Wallingford led twenty-four cavalrymen to the crossing, but the Indians were gone before they arrived.

The teamsters of that train reported finding the debris of a wagon train a few miles south of Cimarron Crossing that had been attacked and destroyed by fire. They found and buried the bodies of fifteen people, including two women, who had been killed and mutilated by Indians.

On the morning of September 2 an ambulance with a large white flag approached Fort Dodge from the southeast across the river. It was Arapaho Chief Little Raven. He had fastened a wagon cover to a long tipi pole and tied it upright to his ambulance, which the government had given him the previous year. Little Raven, accompanied by Powder Face and Spotted Wolf, met with Lieutenant Colonel Sully and asked to come to the post for a conference. Since General Sheridan was expected later the same day, the Arapahos were requested to camp across the river and wait for him.

The following day Sheridan met Little Raven, who declared the Arapahos were peaceful and had not participated in any of the recent attacks. He told Sheridan he was taking his people to the reservation. Little Raven was a peace leader and hoped to avoid conflict with the army.

On September 2, the same day Little Raven and General Sheridan arrived at Fort Dodge, four soldiers from the post—Corporal James Goodwin and Privates John O'Donnell, Charles Hartman, and Charles Tolan, all members of Troop B, Seventh Cavalry—were attacked by Indians at Little Coon Creek about thirteen miles east of the fort. They were returning from taking a wagon load of wood to the soldiers guarding Big Coon Creek stage station. They would surely have perished had not two soldiers from the fort come upon the scene, provided assistance, and obtained reinforcements. Soldiers from Fort Dodge rescued them.

The Indians became more audacious. A party of Comanches and Kiowas attacked Fort Dodge on September 3 while General Sheridan was there. It was rare for Indians to strike a concentration of soldiers, but it may have been an act of desperation designed to disable the garrison. It did not work. The attackers were driven off after a fierce battle, during which four soldiers were killed and seventeen wounded. The Indian losses were unknown. On the same day a Mexican wagon train was attacked near the post by Cheyennes and Arapahos. The Indians killed and scalped sixteen Mexican teamsters.

Sully's expedition left Fort Dodge on September 7, crossed the river about a mile west of the post, and marched to the Cimarron. Before Sheridan left Fort Dodge on September 9 to return to Fort Hays, he sent

George Armstrong Custer, 1839–1876, graduated from West Point in 1861 and was appointed second lieutenant in the Second Cavalry. He compiled a distinguished Civil War record and was awarded the rank of brevet major general. When the Seventh Cavalry was organized after the Civil War, Custer was appointed lieutenant colonel, the rank he held until his death at the Little Bighorn. Custer participated in General Hancock's expedition, 1867, and led troops in the field during General Sheridan's winter campaign, 1868–1869. He passed through Fort Dodge on his way to and from that expedition.

scouts L. H. Funcher and Aaron Dickinson to report to Sully. The two men were never heard from again, and it was presumed they were killed by Indians. At Fort Hays, Sheridan completed arrangements for his winter campaign. He requested more troops for the department, and he recalled George A. Custer to duty, before his year of suspension expired, to lead the Seventh Cavalry in the field.

In an effort to deal with hostile Indians until reinforcements arrived, Sheridan had earlier authorized Major George A. Forsyth, Ninth Cavalry, to raise a company of frontier scouts to pursue Indians along the Smoky Hill Route. Forsyth's scouts were attacked on September 17 on the

The photo on the facing page shows General Custer in the opening of his Sibley tent (note similarity of this army tent to the Indians' tipis) near Fort Dodge in the fall of 1868 (Custer was then encamped about ten miles from the fort). Custer usually kept many hounds with him, some of which are shown here along with a pelican that was part of Custer's "zoo" at the time. The above photo, taken the same day, shows Custer beside his tent with the Osage scouts who accompanied his campaign seated in the foreground (note the pelican at right).

Arikaree Fork of the Republican River. Forsyth's subaltern, Lieutenant Frederick H. Beecher, was killed there, along with the unit's surgeon and several scouts. The engagement became known as the Battle of Beecher Island. Forsyth's Scouts had failed to deter Indian resistance.

Sully accomplished little more south of the Arkansas. At the Cimarron River he discovered the Indians had received advance warning and moved farther south. The troops followed, and the Indians threatened them constantly, fighting a rear-guard action to provide time for their families to reach safety. There were a few skirmishes. The Indians managed to drive off some horses and mules. After several minor engagements, the Indians made a determined attack on September 15. The troops were nearly drawn into an ambush, and both sides suffered casualties in the battle.

Fearing another assault, Sully lost his nerve and retreated back toward Fort Dodge. His excuse was that the supplies were running low, and he moved north to wait for a supply train. He established a camp on Bluff Creek about sixty-five miles south-southeast of the fort to await more supplies and reinforcements. Sully was injured in a minor accident

Samuel Johnson Crawford, 1835–1913, came to Kansas Territory in 1859 as a young attorney. During the Civil War he served as captain of the Second Kansas Cavalry and colonel of the Eighty-third U.S. Colored Infantry. He resigned from the service in 1864 when he was elected governor of Kansas, and he was reelected in 1866. In 1867 he authorized the Eighteenth Kansas Cavalry to fight Indians in northwest Kansas. He resigned as governor on November 4, 1868, to assume command of the Nineteenth Kansas Cavalry, which participated in the winter campaign, 1868–1869.

and returned to Fort Dodge for medical treatment. On the evening of September 30 Sully and his escort camped a few miles down river from Fort Dodge, planning to go on to the fort the next day.

About eight o'clock the next morning a band of Indians attacked Sully's camp. They had dashed over the bluffs from the north and, after firing a number of shots into the camp, fled eastward on the Wet Route of the Santa Fe Trail. Troops were mounted and sent in pursuit. After traveling about fifteen miles the soldiers came upon a train of seventy-five wagons that was under attack. When the soldiers appeared the Indians disappeared. They had killed two Mexican teamsters, scalped one of them, and wounded two others. The Indians escaped with several mules and about eight hundred cans of corn and tomatoes from the wagons. The soldiers accompanied the wagon train to Fort Dodge, where they arrived during the afternoon.

An empty supply train from the Bluff Creek camp arrived at Fort Dodge that evening. The escort with the train had seen several parties of Indians that day and fought a brief skirmish with a few of them during the afternoon. There were no casualties.

About 9:00 P.M. gunfire was heard across the river from the post, where a company of cavalry was in camp. The alarm was sounded, and the garrison rolled out to prepare for a possible attack. The excitement proved to be a false alarm. One cow was shot.

Sully arrived at Fort Dodge on October 2, reported as being sick, and remained until October 28 when he left to go to Fort Hays. He recommended that a depot for supplies be located approximately one hundred miles south of Fort Dodge to serve the expedition. Camp Supply was established on November 18, 1868, at the confluence of Wolf Creek and Beaver Creek, which together became the North Fork of the Canadian River. The name of the post was changed to Fort Supply in 1878, and it was occupied until 1895.

Lieutenant Colonel George A. Custer, Sully's replacement to command the troops south of the Arkansas, arrived at Fort Dodge on October 9 and left a short time later to join the troops at Bluff Creek camp. Sully was back at Fort Dodge on November 12, on his way to resume command of the expedition. Later, after a dispute between Sully and Custer caused Sheridan to again place Custer in command, Sully returned to Fort Dodge on November 27 and left the following day to go to Fort Harker.

Meanwhile, in October, Custer had encountered stiff Indian resistance. A few days after taking command in the field he was ordered to move his troops north and scour the region between Medicine Lodge Creek and Fort Zarah while supplies and reinforcements accumulated at Fort Dodge for a second move against the Indian encampments believed to be located near the Canadian River. Custer's command encountered a few small bands of Indians in the assigned area, but no villages were located. Several skirmishes occurred, and two Indians were reported killed. On October 21 these troops went into camp on the Arkansas River about ten miles below Fort Dodge. There Custer drilled them constantly in preparation for the winter campaign.

On October 15 General Sheridan informed General Sherman about recent developments. He stated that ninety-two Indians had been killed, but "no villages have as yet been destroyed, and no large amount of stock captured." During the same time seventy-nine citizens had been killed by Indians, and the army had lost six soldiers killed and ten wounded and five scouts killed and sixteen wounded. He estimated that the Indians had stolen more than five thousand head of livestock in western Kansas and eastern Colorado Territory. Many settlements, farms, and ranches had been abandoned.

Sheridan expressed his hope for the winter campaign: "As soon as the failure of the grass and the cold weather forces the scattered bands to come together to winter in the milder latitudes south of the Arkansas, a movement of troops will then take place, . . . which I hope will be successful in gaining a permanent peace."

This sketch of General Philip H. Sheridan on the march to the winter campaign appeared in Harper's Weekly, *December 5, 1868.*

Sherman approved of Sheridan's plans: "You may now go ahead in your own way, and I will back you with my whole authority, and stand between you and any efforts that may be attempted in your rear to restrain your purpose or check your troops."

Sheridan completed arrangements for the winter campaign by early November. Three columns of troops, one each from Fort Dodge, Fort Lyon, and Fort Bascom, New Mexico, were to converge on the winter camps of the tribes in present western Oklahoma. Supplies for the troops were shipped by wagon train from Hays City through Fort Dodge to Camp Supply for distribution in the field. The troops left at Fort Dodge were to safeguard the route and wagon trains.

Kansas governor Samuel J. Crawford had called up a battalion of Kansas volunteers in August 1868, comprising five companies of militia known as the Frontier Battalion commanded by Major George B. Jenness. This unit was later expanded into a twelve-company volunteer regiment of cavalry, the Nineteenth Kansas, which was organized and outfitted at Topeka. Crawford resigned his office as governor to take command of the regiment. These troops joined the winter campaign. They had a difficult time, ran out of provisions, became lost, and nearly starved before being rescued. They finally reached Camp Supply.

Although the tribes were reported to be moving south for the winter, raids continued along the Santa Fe Trail. On October 26, 1868, unidentified Indians attacked the herders watching livestock from Fort Dodge, grazing south of the river. Several head of livestock were killed, but none of the herders was injured. A couple of shells from a Parrott gun, a three-inch rifled cannon, were fired at the Indians, causing them to break off the attack. A detail of infantry crossed the river and scoured the sand hills but no Indians were found.

On November 12, as previously noted, Sully left Fort Dodge to launch the winter campaign. He joined Custer and his troops several miles south of the post. The long column of troops was accompanied by a supply train of four hundred wagons. They marched quickly to Camp Supply, where the soldiers began erecting buildings and awaited orders to march to the Indian villages.

Sheridan arrived at Fort Dodge on November 17 and left the next day for Camp Supply. Sheridan may have thought the Indians had moved south of the Arkansas, but the day after he left Fort Dodge nearly one hundred Indians raided within a half mile of the post. They attempted to drive off the herd of cattle owned by the beef contractor and the mules from a supply train under command of Second Lieutenant Quintin Campbell, Fifth Infantry. The attack was not a surprise, however, because scouts from the fort had apprised everyone that Indians were near.

The raid occurred within sight of the post, and Second Lieutenant Philip Reade, Third Infantry, directed Ordnance Sergeant John C. Hughes to fire a couple of shots from the Parrott gun at the Indians, who quickly fled from the scene. None of the livestock was lost. Several soldiers and scouts from the post pursued the raiders for seven miles, where the Indians set fire to the grass, crossed the Arkansas River, and escaped. The soldiers believed they had killed two of the Indians.

On the same day Ralph Morrison, a citizen visiting at Fort Dodge, ignored the warnings of Indians close by and went hunting alone. He was captured by Indians believed to be Cheyennes, killed, and scalped, within a mile of the fort. His remains were found by troops returning from the pursuit of those who tried to steal the livestock. William S. Soule, a photographer who was working at the time in the post trader's store, photographed Morrison's body before it was brought to the post for burial.

Before Sheridan left Fort Dodge he sent two scouts to find a portion of the Nineteenth Kansas Cavalry and report back to him. The scouts were not heard from again. More than two weeks later one of the supply trains found their remains under a tree that had almost been cut down by bullets. The scouts had been caught by Indians and had stood them off until they ran out of ammunition.

This photograph by William S. Soule, taken November 19, 1868, shows the scalped body of Ralph Morrison a short time after he was killed and scalped by Indians within a mile of Fort Dodge. The others in the photo are Second Lieutenant Philip Reade, Third Infantry, and John O. Austin, chief of scouts at Fort Dodge. Soule was a professional photographer before the Civil War, had served in that war, and was a clerk in the post trader's store at Fort Dodge in 1868. A woodcut based on this photograph was published in Harper's Weekly, *January 16, 1869.*

Several engagements occurred during the winter campaign, but the most important was the Battle of the Washita, November 27, 1868. Custer and the Seventh Cavalry attacked Black Kettle's village of Cheyennes. Black Kettle, an advocate for peace with the United States who had survived the Sand Creek Massacre four years earlier, was killed along with more than one hundred others. The soldiers lost twenty-two killed and fourteen wounded. They captured the village, took fifty-three prisoners, and destroyed some eight hundred captured horses. The prisoners were taken to Fort Hays until released the following summer.

Fort Dodge was an important link in the supply route for the winter campaign, serving as a depot for materials destined for Camp Supply and the expedition. Great quantities of rations and supplies were required, as a few examples will show. Before the campaign began, four hundred thousand rations were stored at Fort Dodge to be delivered to Camp Supply as needed. As previously noted, a supply train of four hundred wagons

Lieutenant Colonel George A. Custer and his command on the march through a snowstorm to attack Black Kettle's Cheyenne village on the Washita River on November 27, 1868. The supplies for the winter campaign came to Fort Hays by rail, to Fort Dodge by wagon train, and were distributed to troops in the field and to Camp Supply from Fort Dodge. This sketch appeared in Harper's Weekly, *December 19, 1868.*

accompanied Lieutenant Alfred Sully's command on the march to Camp Supply. Captain Henry Inman, quartermaster department, was in charge of the supply trains for the winter campaign.

Late in November Inman and an escort accompanied 250 wagons back to Fort Dodge for more supplies. They returned to Camp Supply on December 5. On December 14, 1868, Inman arrived at Fort Dodge from Camp Supply with 180 wagons for more supplies This train and its escort also brought the fifty-three captives from the Battle of the Washita and fourteen sick and wounded soldiers. On December 18 Inman and his escort left Fort Dodge with 250 wagons loaded with stores for Camp Supply. On December 28 he returned to Fort Dodge with 270 empty wagons, escorted by nearly four hundred soldiers. And so it went until the need for provisions at Camp Supply was filled.

The winter campaign ended in the spring of 1869. Custer and the Seventh Cavalry and Nineteenth Kansas Cavalry arrived at Fort Dodge on their return to Fort Hays on April 2, 1869. They camped for the night and proceeded on the next day.

Provisions for Camp Supply continued to flow through Fort Dodge for the next several years. Troops from both posts protected the Fort Dodge–Camp Supply Trail and manned two redoubts established in 1871, one near Bear Creek thirty-five miles south of Fort Dodge and the other near the Cimarron River thirty-eight miles north of Camp Supply. The two forts had a close relationship until Fort Dodge was closed in 1882.

Black Kettle was a leading peace chief of the Southern Cheyennes. He signed treaties and urged accord with Euro-Americans, believing his people would be destroyed in a war with the U.S. Army. His village at Sand Creek, Colorado, was attacked by Colonel John M. Chivington in November 1864. Black Kettle survived and supported the treaties of the Little Arkansas, 1865, and Medicine Lodge, 1867. He and his wife, as well as many members of his band, died at the Battle of the Washita in November 1868. His life and death exemplified the tragedy of the Plains Indian wars.

Henry Inman, 1837–1899, enlisted in the army in 1857 and later was commissioned an officer. He was assigned to the quartermaster department during the Civil War. After the war he served as a quartermaster in Kansas and directed the supply operations for the winter campaign, 1868–1869. He was dismissed from the service in 1872 because of chronic discrepancies in his accounts. He later entered journalism, worked for various Kansas newspapers, and wrote several books (some of questionable veracity).

70

7

Mission Completed: Indian Defeat and Removal to Reservations

ecause most of the Indians accepted their reservation assignments after the winter campaign, it was the beginning of the end of Indian occupation of western Kansas. General Sheridan was promoted to division commander in March 1869. Sherman had been promoted to commanding general of the army when Ulysses S. Grant became president. The Department of the Missouri was commanded by Major General John M. Schofield until April 1870 when General John Pope assumed that office. By that time the "Indian problem" in western Kansas was largely resolved.

The winter campaign had produced a remarkable decrease in Indian hostilities along the Santa Fe Trail. The Cheyenne Dog Soldiers under Tall Bull, who had refused to go to the reservation, were defeated the following summer in Colorado Territory. After that occasional raids occurred, but for the most part the overland routes and settlements on the Central Plains were safer than at any time in three decades. But more Indian wars remained to be fought on the Southern and Northern Plains.

The number of settlers moving into western Kansas increased markedly during the 1870s and early 1880s. The railroads built across the state, the buffalo were slaughtered, the cattle drives from Texas reached their zenith, and farming and ranching expanded rapidly. Some former soldiers and civilian employees at Fort Dodge became citizens of Dodge City, and other soldiers took advantage of the homestead law to acquire property in the region on which they settled after their term of service.

Agriculture faced good times and bad, including grasshoppers and drought, but the Indian threats were virtually gone. Fort Dodge had little contact with hostile Indians again, except for a few occasions when restless tribesmen broke away from their reservation. Indians who took a less belligerent attitude after the winter campaign sometimes visited the post.

The only reported Indian hostility in the area during 1870 was an attack on an army ambulance between Fort Hays and Fort Dodge in March. No record of Indian hostilities around Fort Dodge was found for the year 1871. In the spring of 1872 a party of seven Kiowas ran off the mules of a wagon train traveling between Camp Supply and Fort Dodge. On May 22, 1872, two privates of Company G, Sixth Cavalry, serving as couriers were attacked between Fort Dodge and Camp Supply by a small party of Indians. Alexander Christopher was killed, and Henry Meussman was seriously wounded and died on June 1 at Camp Supply. The Indians took their horses, arms, and equipment.

In October 1872 a small party of peaceful Northern Cheyennes was returning home after visiting the Southern Cheyennes. They were fired upon by buffalo hunters who apparently considered all Indians to be hostile, and one Cheyenne was killed near Walnut Creek some sixty miles from Fort Dodge. To avenge this unprovoked attack, these Indians later killed three men and captured one woman. Then they returned to their homeland without further troubles.

During 1872 the Atchison, Topeka and Santa Fe Railroad built westward to Dodge City and beyond. The troops at the post helped guard construction crews and newly established railroad stations. The railroad delivered supplies to the post, bringing an end to military freighting over the Fort Hays–Fort Dodge Trail, which troops from the post had been helping guard from possible Indian attacks.

Problems other than Indians also occupied troops at Fort Dodge. On August 8, 1872, a detail of Company G, Sixth Cavalry, comprising Sergeant Pettice L. Beatty, Corporal Samuel M. Kohr, and twelve privates, was sent in pursuit of a gang of thieves who had stolen horses from the railroad and robbed two soldiers. The detail followed their trail for nearly three hundred miles and overtook the outlaws in New Mexico Territory, approximately one hundred miles southwest of Fort Lyon, Colorado Territory. The soldiers attacked at night on August 16 and killed one, captured another, and recovered seventeen horses and mules. They returned to Fort Dodge on August 28.

On November 4, 1874, Second Lieutenant Robert Hanna, Sixth Cavalry, and ten privates and a guide were sent by rail to Great Bend,

Robert Hanna, 1848–1908, graduated from West Point in 1872. He was a second lieutenant of Company B, Sixth Cavalry, at Fort Dodge in 1874 when he led a detachment in pursuit of horse thieves. He transferred to Camp Supply soon after that expedition and later served against the Apaches in Arizona. He rose to the rank of captain in 1888, a position he held when this photograph was taken. He retired from service in 1891.

Kansas, to pursue thieves who had stolen horses from a band of peaceful Arapahos near Ellinwood, Kansas. Hanna followed the robbers' trail to the Fort Hays–Fort Larned Trail north of Larned where the thieves' tracks were obliterated by cattle trails. The soldiers continued to search and met a party of buffalo hunters who reported seeing three men with a herd of horses near the Fort Hays–Fort Dodge Trail. Hanna headed in that direction and picked up the trail again near Duncan's Crossing on that route. The troops caught up with bandits on November 10 between the Pawnee and Arkansas Rivers, and the thieves gave battle. Hanna's detachment opened fire, wounding two in an engagement that lasted nearly two hours. They recovered most of the horses and one mule. Hanna's horse was killed, and one of the soldiers, Alfred Skilton, was wounded. The detail returned to Fort Dodge the next day, having traveled 208 miles on the excursion. Other troops from the post continued to protect the railroad.

The effect of the railroad on Fort Dodge was explained by the post surgeon in 1875: "The completion of the railroad to this post has given it the importance formerly attached to Fort Hays. It is now the point from which the Cheyenne, Arapahoe, Kiowa, and Comanche Indians are watched." Also, when the railroad arrived at Dodge City, originally called

With the arrival of the railroad at Dodge City, originally known as Buffalo City, the town became a center for buffalo hunters who eliminated the vast herds within a few years. These sketches by S.E. Waller, entitled A Day's "Still Hunting" After Buffalo, *were published in* Harpers' Weekly, *May 10, 1877.*

Buffalo City, it became the center for buffalo hunters who quickly elimi-nated the large herds in the Central and Southern Plains. This slaughter removed the commissary on which Plains Indians had depended for more than a century. It was encouraged by military leaders and made it impos-sible for the Indians to sustain their traditional way of life. General Philip Sheridan testified before the Texas legislature in 1875 that the buffalo hunters "have done more in the last two years, and will do in the next year, more to settle the vexed Indian question than the entire regular army has done in the last thirty years." Only a few officers protested.

Dodge City was the center of the buffalo slaughter, providing every-thing the hunters needed and buying and shipping hides and meat. Robert Wright claimed he shipped 200,000 buffalo hides during his first year in business in the new town. The next year he also bought and sold one and a half million pounds of buffalo meat. From 1872 through 1874 an estimated 850,000 buffalo hides were shipped from Dodge City.

The buffalo were eliminated in the region. Many reservation Indians, who hoped to continue traditional hunting, were outraged. Unlike many of his fellow officers, Major Richard I. Dodge, commanding Fort Dodge, expressed understanding and sympathy for the situation. He explained in October 1873 that the hunters were "slaughtering the Buffalo by hundreds and thousands, immediately in the presence, and almost in the very camps of the Indians." He warned the results of this slaughter would lead to disaster. The Indians, he predicted, would try to "drive out the hunters, probably with bloodshed, which will inaugurate a war." In addition, the reduction of the buffalo herds would result in the failure of the Indians "to obtain their winter's supply of meat and skins, which means to them starvation, or extreme suffering."

In the spring of 1874 buffalo hunters moved south from Dodge City to establish a base of operations near the old trading post of Adobe Walls on the Canadian River in Texas. From there they could finish off the herds of that region. Some Comanches, Kiowas, and Cheyennes, frustrated with reservation life and fortified by whiskey provided by illegal traders, were determined to strike back. They began to raid along the Fort Dodge–Camp Supply Trail and into southern Kansas.

In April 1874 a small band of Cheyennes, accompanied by a white man known as "Frenchy," stole livestock from settlers along Medicine Lodge Creek some sixty miles southeast of Fort Dodge. Captain Tullius C. Tupper and his Company G, Sixth Cavalry, stationed at the fort, were scouting in the area at the time and pursued the thieves. They recovered fifty-three cattle, sixteen horses, and two mules, and returned these to their owners. The Indians were forced to return to their reservation. Frenchy was James French, an itinerant miscreant who was living with Little Robe's band of Southern Cheyennes, supplying them with whiskey. The Cheyennes ran him out of their camp in June, charging that Frenchy had been spying on them. Frenchy became a skinner for buffalo hunter Billy Dixon and was among the hunters attacked at Adobe Walls a few days later.

In June 1874 a party of Kiowas killed and mutilated two buffalo hunters within fifteen miles of Adobe Walls. A small party of Indians attacked the mail party from Camp Supply about twenty miles north of that post, wounding one man who was treated upon his arrival at Fort Dodge. More troops from the post were sent to scout the region south of the Arkansas River. Additional soldiers were sent to guard railroad stations east and west of the post and to reinforce the redoubts on the Fort

The buffalo slaughter, encouraged by some army officers, made it impossible for the Plains tribes to continue their old ways of life. The once mobile tribes, deprived of their commissary, had no choice but to reside on the reservations as wards of the government. This sketch of soldiers "Counting the Tongues" of their kill appeared in Harper's Weekly, *June 6, 1867.*

Dodge–Camp Supply Trail. The Indians continued to raid at random, killing four citizens in the Medicine Lodge area. Several small parties, some with military escorts, were threatened while traveling between Fort Dodge and Camp Supply. Some Indians were determined to attack the headquarters of the buffalo hunters. A combined force of 250 to 300 Kiowas, Comanches, and Cheyennes charged Adobe Walls on June 27. They failed to dislodge the hunters, but the war that Major Dodge had feared soon followed.

Indian resistance increased in western Kansas. On July 2 unidentified Indians burned a railroad bridge about thirty miles west of Fort Dodge. Troops were dispatched but failed to find the perpetrators. Several railroad stations were raided farther west into Colorado Territory, as far as Granada. Soldiers were placed at each railroad station from Kinsley, Kansas, 30 miles east of Fort Dodge, to Granada, 130 miles west.

Several companies of cavalry were ordered out to scout the region north and south of the Arkansas and turn back the Indians to their reservations if possible. The Atchison, Topeka and Santa Fe Railroad made available a spe-

Buffalo hides were shipped by rail from Dodge City in huge quantities, as shown in this illustration.

cial train, at no cost to the army, equipped to carry cavalrymen and their horses, which could be loaded or unloaded at any location. The train operated under the direction of the commanding officer at Fort Dodge. Despite these efforts, some Indians moved farther north to continue raiding. The troops in the field were directed to consider all Indians as hostile and to "strike them hard." This did not happen, however, because the soldiers could not find the Indians, who continued their hit-and-run tactic.

Several parties of Cheyennes were active in western Kansas. Among their targets was Duncan's Ranch at the crossing of Pawnee Fork on the Fort Hays–Fort Dodge Trail, struck on July 23. On August 15 Indians killed four citizens near the site of old Fort Aubrey. The same day Indians burned a railroad bridge near Pierceville, located on the railroad about forty-five miles west of Fort Dodge. A noted incident, committed while the Cheyennes were moving north from Indian Territory, was an attack on a survey party some fifty miles southwest of Fort Dodge in present Meade County on August 24, 1874. The encounter became known as the Lone Tree Massacre.

The contract to survey and mark township and section boundaries in the region was held by three men from eastern Kansas: Oliver Francis Short, L. A. Thrasher, and Abram Cutler. Short led the survey party of twenty-two men and several wagons loaded with equipment and supplies. Among the assistants were Short's sons, Harold C. and Daniel Truman. The entire party camped together near a lone cottonwood tree not far from Crooked Creek and close to a small lake. They divided into three groups to work during the daytime, leaving a few men to protect the camp, hunt, and cook the meals.

It was known that hostile Indians were in the area, and Oliver Short had requested a military escort. This was not provided, apparently because troops were not available at the time. At least six companies of troops from Fort Dodge were scouting to the south on the way to join an expedition against the Indians, and it was believed they would deter any threats. A few days before the attack, Oliver Short wrote to his wife, "A great many soldiers have gone below so we have no apprehensions of Indians, still we shall keep a careful watching." They were not careful enough, however. On August 24 a party of some twenty-five Cheyennes surprised Short's crew of six, and a running fight covered almost four miles before all members of this crew were killed. It was believed several Indians were killed. The remains of the surveyors were found by another crew two days later and buried near the lone tree. The survey was abandoned and the remainder of the party hurried to Fort Dodge. The remains of the six who died were removed to eastern cemeteries the following year.

A party of Cheyennes led by Gray Beard and Medicine Water perpetrated several raids during the summer of 1874, including an attack on John and Lydia German and their seven children near Fort Wallace in September 1874. The Cheyennes raided farther north in western Kansas before returning to Indian Territory. On their return, on September 15, some of them attacked the railroad settlement of Pierceville and burned the only house in town. The Pierceville post office was closed as a result, and it was not reestablished until 1878. As raiding continued, the army confronted the hostile tribesmen. The conflict spread and developed into the Red River War, 1874–1875, which saw the final subjugation of the Indians of the Southern Plains.

The Red River War was fought, in part, by the Indian Territory Expedition, organized by Colonel Nelson A. Miles, Fifth Infantry, at Fort Dodge in July 1874, and later turned into another winter campaign on the Southern Plains. General Sheridan visited Fort Dodge on November 4, inspected the post, and left the same day. The post was a vital link in the supply line for the troops in the field.

Troops from Fort Dodge remained stationed at towns along the Atchison, Topeka and Santa Fe line to protect the route of supply.

Richard Irving Dodge commanded Fort Dodge during portions of 1872 and 1873 and was one of the founders of Dodge City. A native of North Carolina, Dodge graduated from West Point in 1848 and was assigned to the Eighth Infantry, in which he served until after the Civil War, rising to the rank of major. In 1866 he transferred to the Third Infantry, his regiment at the time he commanded Fort Dodge. He left Fort Dodge when he was promoted to lieutenant colonel of the Twenty-third Infantry in 1873. He was promoted to colonel and served as General William T. Sherman's aide-de-camp, 1881–1882. He served as colonel of the Eleventh Infantry from 1882 until his retirement in May 1891. Dodge died June 15, 1895. He was the author of several books, including The Plains of the Great West *(1877) and* Our Wild Indians *(1881).*

Provisions were again sent south from Fort Dodge to Camp Supply in huge quantities. On October 24 a wagon train departed for Camp Supply with 35,434 pounds of corn and 11,310 pounds of subsistence stores. The following day another caravan departed for Camp Supply with 73,109 pounds of subsistence stores, 24,471 pounds of corn, and 852 pounds of medical stores. On October 27 twelve wagons started for Camp Supply with 38,000 pounds of corn and 2,000 pounds of quartermaster stores. The next day an ox train left with 64,329 pounds of corn and 2,503 pounds of quartermaster stores. On November 3 a contract train left for Camp Supply with 1,026 pounds of lumber, 28,250 pounds of shingles, and 14,198 pounds of bricks. Other trains followed as quickly as possible. The freight contractors, including Post Trader Robert Wright, were unable to fulfill the requirements of the campaign, and the army was forced to haul provisions. Officers from Fort Dodge scoured the countryside along the railroad in each direction, as far east as Newton, Kansas, and west to Granada, "to procure transportation at any price." An officer seeking draft animals reported from Fort Dodge,

Major Charles Elmer Compton, Sixth Cavalry, commanded Fort Dodge, November 1873–August 1874 and February–August 1875. He entered the service early in the Civil War as a sergeant in the First Iowa Infantry. He became captain of the Eleventh Iowa Infantry in October 1861 and was commissioned a major of the Forty-seventh U.S. Colored Infantry in 1863 and a lieutenant colonel of the Fifty-third U.S. Colored Infantry in 1864. After the war he was appointed major of the Fortieth Infantry and transferred to the Sixth Cavalry in 1869, the rank he held at Fort Dodge. He became lieutenant colonel of the Fifth Cavalry in 1879 and colonel of the Fourth Cavalry in 1887. He was promoted to brigadier general in 1898 and retired the following year. He received brevet ranks for gallant and meritorious service at Mobile, Alabama (1864), and for leading a cavalry battalion in a successful charge against Indians on the Red River in Texas in 1874.

"Everything possible is being done to get teams, but they are not here, and must be got from a distance."

Within two weeks draft animals and wagons were engaged and more were procured in the weeks that followed. More than three hundred mules and fifty wagons were sent to Fort Dodge from the Department of Dakota. Except for delays caused by snowstorms, the flow of provisions continued to Camp Supply and to the Indian Territory Expedition in the field. As quickly as possible the empty wagons returned to Dodge City to load again. Captain James H. Bradford, Nineteenth Infantry, commanding the post, reported that between November 25, 1874, and February 10, 1875, more than two million pounds of supplies (80 percent was grain for the cavalry horses) had been freighted from Fort Dodge and Dodge City to Camp Supply. This supplying effort required all the men and equipment

Philip H. Remington, photo taken when he was a cadet at West Point just prior to the Civil War. Assigned as a second lieutenant to the Eighth Infantry in 1861 and quickly promoted to first lieutenant, Remington served as regimental adjutant during much of the Civil War. He was promoted to captain in 1866 and transferred to the Nineteenth Infantry in 1869, in which capacity he served at Fort Dodge in 1878. He commanded Fort Dodge briefly following the death of Lieutenant Colonel W. H. Lewis in September 1878. Remington retired in February 1891 and died in December the same year.

available, and it was facilitated under difficult winter conditions. Escorts for the wagon trains were required because of Indian threats.

Although Indians occasionally were seen in Kansas and a small party of Cheyennes was severely defeated on Sappa Creek in the northwest part of the state on April 23, 1875, most engagements of the Red River War occurred far south of Fort Dodge. When all the recalcitrant tribesmen surrendered or were conquered in 1875, the Southern Plains Indians' traditional way of life was finished. They begrudgingly acknowledged their defeat and began to accommodate themselves to the circumstances imposed upon them by the victors. After the war buffalo hunters completed the slaughter of the buffalo in the region within three years. The Indians were dependent on the government for survival. Reservation life was neither pleasant nor prosperous, but their resistance was broken. Except for a rare escape from the reservations, western Kansas was free from Indian attack.

The "last Indian raid" in Kansas occurred in September 1878 when some three hundred Northern Cheyennes, under Chiefs Dull Knife and Little Wolf, fled the reservation in Indian Territory (present Oklahoma) in an attempt to return to their homeland in Montana. The party consisted of about seventy-five men, and the rest were women and children.

81

Cheyenne men who accompanied Dull Knife in 1878, brought back to Dodge City for trial in 1879. This photo was taken in Dodge City, April 30, 1879; bottom row, left to right: Wild Hog, George Reynolds (interpreter), Old Man, and Blacksmith; top row, left to right: Frizzle Hair, Rain in the Face, Crow, and White Antelope; the man above was not identified. According to Robert Wright, the Indians would only be photographed with their interpreter, fearing the camera would shoot them. Their trial was moved from Ford County to Douglas County, and the Indians were released when the prosecutor failed to supply evidence against them. Identification of these individuals varies in other images of this group.

They obtained horses and provisions as they moved north. During the march the Cheyennes scattered over a large area because the men raided and foraged some fifteen to twenty miles on either side of the women and children. Because they ranged over so much territory, it was erroneously assumed by the army and citizens that the band was much larger than it really was.

The troops at Fort Dodge were alerted about the Cheyennes' escape and attempted to capture them. On September 9, 1878, Captain Philip Halsey Remington, Nineteenth Infantry, led his company from the post to Pierceville, about forty-five miles west. They were expected to intercept the Cheyennes, but the soldiers returned to the post on September 13, having seen no signs of them.

The following day a company of Fourth Cavalry that had been scouting for the Cheyennes arrived at Fort Dodge. They picked up provisions and continued their search the next day. They had a skirmish with the Indians near Bear Creek on September 18 and were forced to retreat. The company returned to Fort Dodge on September 19 for reinforcements. Meanwhile, on September 17, a company of infantry left the post by rail for Pierceville to prevent the Cheyennes from crossing the Arkansas River. They returned to the fort on September 22 and reported that the Indians had retreated to the southwest.

A company of infantry arrived at Fort Dodge from Fort Riley on September 18 to help find the Cheyennes. As quickly as possible four companies of troops headed southwest to search for the evasive Indians. These troops attacked the Indians near Sand Creek, a tributary of the Cimarron River, on September 22, and a running battle lasted nearly eight hours. The Indians retreated into the bluffs, from which they escaped during the night. No casualties were reported for this engagement.

On September 25 Lieutenant Colonel William Henry Lewis, commander at Fort Dodge, took three companies to the Cimarron River where three more companies joined his force. They followed the Cheyennes northward and caught up with them on September 27 at Punished Woman's Fork in present Scott County, Kansas. They attacked, but the Indians offered a good defense and escaped again with the loss of one man killed. Lewis and two soldiers were wounded. Lewis, who took a bullet in the thigh severing the femoral artery, died during the night. He was the only commanding officer of a military post to be killed in battle by Indians. Mary Leefe, daughter of the post quartermaster, recalled that the earliest memory from her childhood was the memorial service for Lieutenant Colonel Lewis, when she was six years old.

The Cheyennes escaped other encounters and continued to elude troops. They crossed the Kansas Pacific Railway undetected. In Decatur County, Kansas, the Cheyennes killed nineteen citizens to avenge the killing of twenty-seven Cheyennes by soldiers at Sappa Creek in 1875.

The fleeing Cheyennes proceeded into Nebraska where Dull Knife and Little Wolf split. Dull Knife surrendered his followers at Camp Robinson,

Nebraska, while Little Wolf led the remainder on to Montana. Dull Knife's band was held under guard at Camp Robinson until they broke out and fled the post on January 9, 1879. The soldiers pursued them through the snow and shot nearly half the Cheyennes. The survivors, including Dull Knife, were not sent back to Indian Territory. Some were sent to Dodge City to be tried for murder, but they were later released because of technicalities. Dull Knife's followers later joined Little Wolf and his band, who made it to Montana. In 1884, the year after Dull Knife died, the Northern Cheyennes were granted a permanent reservation on the Tongue River in Montana where the Lame Deer Agency was established.

Fort Dodge was no longer needed to protect the region from Indians after 1878. The post was garrisoned until 1882, but the number of troops stationed there was small and life at the post was routine. General Sheridan recommended in January 1878 that Fort Dodge and other posts on the Plains be abandoned because they were no longer required. The escape of the Cheyennes later that year showed that troops might still be needed to meet emergency situations. By 1882, with no Indian threat remaining in the region, there was general consensus that the post should be closed.

8

Life at the Post

The daily life of soldiers at frontier military posts was generally routine, monotonous, and austere, with occasional periods of excitement and danger. The quarters were plain, hot in summer and cold in winter. The rations seldom varied, and almost every soldier complained about the quality of the food. Each enlisted man had to take a regular turn at guard duty and kitchen police. Much of the day at the post was spent at common labor, erecting and repairing buildings, unloading and loading supplies, herding livestock, hauling garbage, and other fatigue details. The army provided no recreational facilities, although the post sutler or trader offered some amusements, and soldiers had to provide most of their own entertainment during free time. Assignments that took the soldiers away from the post temporarily included escorts for stagecoaches and wagon trains, scouting expeditions, and campaigns against Indians.

Few women were found at military posts, although camp followers were always present nearby. Laundresses, most of whom were married to enlisted soldiers, were the only women that the army recognized as having a reason to live at a military post, with laundresses' quarters provided and established pay scales set for officers and enlisted men who used their services. Military posts had no provisions for officers' wives. They officially were considered to be camp followers. Officer housing was assigned by rank, regardless of marital status, and a single captain, for example, could force a lieutenant with a family from adequate accommodations into a single room or, if nothing else were available, a tent.

With few diversions, the garrison followed a fixed schedule of activities each day. A typical timetable, announced by drums or bugle calls, began with reveille at 5:55 A.M., with assembly for roll call at 6:00. Mess call for breakfast was at 6:15, stable call for mounted troops came at 7:00, and sick call was at 7:30, when those who were ailing reported to the post hospital to be examined by the surgeon and treated if necessary. Fatigue call also sounded at 7:30, and the men were set to work at whatever tasks were assigned. At 8:00 the new guard for the day was called, inspected, and set to work for the next twenty-four hours. Mess call for dinner was at 12:00 noon. Afternoon fatigue call, or call to drill on some days, sounded at 1:00 P.M. Recall from fatigue or drill was at 4:30. An assembly of the troops came at 5:30, followed by the dress parade at 5:40. Supper call sounded at 6:30. The call to quarters ended the day at 9:30, with taps at 10:00.

On Sunday roll call and inspection occurred at 8:00 A.M., with guard mount immediately after inspection. Sometimes a dress parade was called. The remainder of the day was spent at leisure. During the week, when they were not on call, soldiers had free time. They could not leave the post without permission, and they were subject to call as needed.

When a regimental band was stationed at the post, Sunday concerts were presented. The following holidays were observed by suspending all duties except for necessary policing of the post: New Year's Day, George Washington's Birthday, Independence Day, Thanksgiving, and Christmas. An unpleasant break of routine occurred for the burial of a fellow soldier. The daily ritual was occasionally altered by a visit from a famous officer, such as the department commander. Fort Dodge was visited by a number of high-ranking officers, including Generals Hancock, Pope, Sheridan, and Sherman. Colonel (Brevet Brigadier General) Kit Carson spent the night of November 13, 1865, at Fort Dodge. On September 26, 1879, President Rutherford B. Hayes was a guest.

The officers and their families were almost completely separated from the enlisted men, although they did join together occasionally for dances, called "hops," and other entertainment. Musicals and plays, performed by enlisted men with help from officers and their families, were sponsored by officers and their wives. In the evenings it was common for officers and their wives to make formal calls, and the officers frequently entertained their peers with supper and an evening playing cards or some other entertainment. Single officers usually were included in leisure activities. Enlisted men occupied their free time with a variety of activities.

In addition to drinking, gambling, and whoring, the soldiers fished and hunted, participated in sports (horse races and baseball were popular), visited with their fellow soldiers, played musical instruments and sang, and read any mail received and books and periodicals from the post library, which was located in the post adjutant's office. The library included more than 225 volumes of history, biography, and literature, as well as several newspapers and magazines. Many soldiers were illiterate, and those who could read and write frequently read to and wrote for those who could not.

A number of men also learned to read and write in the post school provided for them during evening hours. In June 1879, for example, 26 enlisted men were enrolled of a total of 118 at the post. They were taught reading, writing, grammar, mathematics, history, and geography by Private John F. Guernsey, Company G, Nineteenth Infantry. Guernsey also taught school for children at the post during the daytime, attended by seven children of enlisted men, seven officers' children, and five children of civilians. In November 1879 no classes were held "owing to there being no teacher in the Post."

Until the railroad arrived in 1872, troops at Fort Dodge were isolated. This solitude, coupled with low pay, poor food, drudge labor, and severe discipline, caused many soldiers to desert before their five-year term of enlistment was completed. Desertion was a problem that the army failed to solve until the frontier era was past. As a result, the army was constantly shorthanded.

After the Civil War the entire army lost from 10 percent to more than 20 percent of the enlisted men to desertion each year, and some regiments in some years lost more than 50 percent. A total of 429 soldiers deserted at Fort Dodge from 1866–1882. That was an average of more than 12 percent per year.

Military pay was an important factor. The base pay for privates at the end of the Civil War was sixteen dollars per month, and that was reduced to thirteen dollars in 1870. This resulted in increased desertions, and more than 32 percent of all enlisted men deserted in 1871. During 1871 there were fifty-six desertions at Fort Dodge, the highest for any year. This was more than 23 percent of the average garrison of 238 soldiers. Forty-nine desertions occurred in 1872 from a smaller garrison, when the rate was nearly 27 percent. The rate remained high for several years. Twenty-five desertions occurred in 1882, the year the post was abandoned, from a garrison that averaged only ninety, a desertion rate of nearly 28 percent. Some soldiers had little desire to risk their lives for the compensation provided.

The soldiers received little cash compared with that of civilian laborers, but the government furnished their food, shelter, clothing, medical care, soap, and candles. The salary was used to pay the laundress, tailor, and barber; for personal items purchased at the post trader's store, including tobacco, candy, toothbrush, comb, food, beer, and whiskey; for recreational activities outside the post; and, if any remained, to send home to the family or save for a return to civilian life. Some soldiers did not consider the pay commensurate with the work and risks required, and did not hesitate to desert to escape from the severity of military discipline or to take advantage of other opportunities, such as going to the gold fields in Colorado. (For a table of desertions from the garrison at Fort Dodge, *see* Appendix.)

A constant supply of recruits was required to replenish the losses to desertion, discharge, and medical disability. Many unskilled men and recent immigrants enlisted because they could find no other employment. Some were escaping unpleasant family circumstances, a brush with the law, or civilian obligations. More than a few joined up while under the influence of strong drink and wondered afterward why they had done so. Some foreigners saw the army as place to learn the English language and an avenue to citizenship.

A few of the more literate enlisted men described some of their fellow soldiers as the dregs of society. One private in the Eighth Cavalry proclaimed in the early 1870s that "the Army is composed of the scrapings of Penitentiaries, Jails and everything else combined to make an Army suitable for this Government." A German immigrant who served five years in the Sixteenth Infantry, 1877–1882, recalled that the enlisted men composed "a variety of humanity" and compared one recruit "to Darwin's missing link of some backwoods—just fresh from the farm, with a frame and walk like a cart horse, back like a camel, with brains to match a monkey." The same soldier "found men of intellect and stupidity," including "gamblers, thieves, cutthroats, [and] drunkards" who "under careful training, had produced some of the best soldiers on the frontier."

The enlisted men comprised a wide variety of ethnic origins and a diversity of skills. For example, the *Dodge City Times* of March 27, 1878, reported that among the soldiers of the Nineteenth Infantry stationed at Fort Dodge were eight bookkeepers, a former state legislator, the son of a British nobleman, a former Confederate congressman, two former Confederate officers, a railroad conductor, two medical students, three schoolteachers, four merchants, and a bank president whose bank had failed.

Fort Dodge was established and garrisoned for the first several months by companies of volunteer regiments, some were state and others were federal units, raised during the Civil War. These men spent most

Sutler's Store at Fort Dodge, Kansas, *sketched by Theodore R. Davis, from* Harper's Weekly, *May 25, 1867. The merchandise available at the sutler's store included canned foods (vegetables, fruits, meats, and sea foods), dried fruits, eggs, butter, cheese, crackers, beans, corn meal, flour, baking soda, sugar, coffee, tea, salt, spices, jelly, candy, chocolate, vinegar, molasses, soap, coffee grinders, coffee pots and cups, pots and pans, basins, pitchers, buckets, churns, stoneware, tinware, cookware, glassware, tableware, toothbrushes, cloth, canvas, leather, needles, thread, buttons, beads, laces, pins, awls, nails, scissors, combs, mirrors, razors, cologne, watches, clocks, brooms, brushes, washboards, clothespins, candles, lanterns, lamps, towels, handkerchiefs, underwear, socks, trousers, shirts, skirts, vests, coats, caps, hats, gloves, neckties, shoes, boots, belts, wallets, blankets, pencils, pens, ink, paper, notebooks, playing cards, fish hooks, pocket knives, guns, ammunition, axes, padlocks, matches, tobacco, pipes, cigars, beer, wine, champagne, whiskey, patent medicines, epsom salt, turpentine, rope, horse liniment, horse gear (saddles, halters, bridles, curry combs, etc.), and fodder for livestock.*

of their time constructing the new post and waiting for their term of service to end. The replacements were more volunteers awaiting their release. This turnover of officers and men was not conducive to devotion to duty, particularly care in construction of facilities that they would occupy for only a brief time or not at all.

As regular army units replaced the volunteers in 1866, a degree of stability was established and construction work proceeded from temporary quarters to permanent buildings. When these facilities were completed, living conditions improved. Whenever the size of the garrison exceeded available quarters, the excess lived in tents. The average number of troops stationed at Fort Dodge from month to month varied considerably, from a high of 659 in September and October 1874 to a low of only 36 in October 1882. (For a table of the monthly aggregate garrison, see Appendix.) The monthly average for the seventeen and one-half years the post was active was about two hundred officers and men. Military personnel were supplemented by civilian employees. (For a table of civilians employed at the post, see Appendix.)

The officers, enlisted men, and many civilian laborers received rations, and all were dependent on the post sutler, or post trader after 1867, for many items. The sutler was appointed by the army and enjoyed a monopoly of trade at the military post. In return the sutler paid a fee, usually so much per soldier, and those tolls went into a post fund to provide items for the troops that the military budget did not supply, such as subscriptions to newspapers and magazines, books for the post library, music for the band, and song books.

The sutler's store was like a general store, offering almost everything people needed. On March 30, 1865, the same day that he issued the order to establish Fort Dodge, Colonel James H. Ford offered the position of post sutler to the partnership of Crane and Ladd. Jesse H. Crane had been in charge of the sutler's store at Fort Larned since 1859, and James William Ladd was one of his employees. Crane owned the sutler's store at Fort Larned in partnership with Theodore Weichselbaum, postmaster at Ogden, Kansas, who was engaged in freighting supplies to military posts, contracting to furnish hay and wood for the army, trading with Indians, and operating sutlers' stores at several other military posts. He later operated a brewery at Ogden and distributed beer to towns and forts. Weichselbaum purchased Ladd's interest in the sutler's store at Fort Dodge in late 1866. Crane sold his share to John E. Tappen, after which the business was known as Tappen and Weichselbaum.

Initially, however, Ladd oversaw the business of Crane and Ladd at Fort Dodge, aided by two clerks. They took two wagons loaded with merchandise from Fort Larned on May 3 and arrived at Fort Dodge at 4:00 P.M. the following day. Ladd recorded in his diary that they "Sold a few goods off the wagons" the same day. The next day they erected a Sibley tent to serve as the sutler's store and "Did a good trade" even though it

"Rained all day till 4 o'clock P.M." The following day Ladd recorded, "We were very busy selling goods to the Soldiers on credit." Business was apparently good. On May 12 Ladd sent his wagons to Fort Larned for more commodities, and they returned one week later. On May 29 the wagons again headed to Fort Larned for more provisions.

On May 13 Ladd erected an army wall tent as an addition to the store. Two days later a severe hail storm with strong winds struck, and Ladd wrote, "My tents came very near going down." He erected a sod building for his store as quickly as possible. He hired laborers to cut the sod for one dollar per hundred pieces. On May 31 he recorded, "I have the walls of my new store finished." Completion was apparently delayed by Indian troubles, and Ladd recorded on July 4, 1865, that he "bought Sergt. Youngs house & moved my store into it from the tent." That was a temporary alternative to the tents. On August 24 he wrote, "We moved into our new store on the north side of the road."

On June 12, as previously noted, two of Ladd's employees were killed by Indians. Christopher Ladd, a brother, and Lyman Fargo soon arrived to help with the store. James Ladd went with wagons to Fort Larned in late July to acquire more merchandise. On August 26 another wagon train of "new goods" arrived. Two days later James Ladd recorded, "Trade is very good yesterday & today we have taken about $2000 in cash." Later the same week he noted that "One day this week we sold $1500.00 worth of goods." The sutler's store was a lucrative monopoly. The amount of stock carried was not revealed, although James Ladd noted in his diary on November 3, 1865, that Theodore Weichselbaum's wagons had that day delivered "about $12000.00 worth" of "new goods" for the store.

James Ladd left Fort Dodge to attend the Indian council at the mouth of the Little Arkansas River in October 1865. He was appointed postmaster at Fort Dodge in November 1865. On November 9 he "Moved the Post Office for Hdqrs to the store & put a letter box on the door." On November 13 Kit Carson "called at the store—took supper with us and spent the evening at the store." Ladd continued to make improvements, adding a stable and digging a well. On Christmas day 1865 he "Had a party of all the officers of all the post at my room in the store—Had fruit &c and a good time."

The sutler's store continued to be a profitable enterprise. During the summer of 1866 the enlisted men at Fort Dodge complained that Ladd was abusing his appointment by charging excessive prices for his stock. In August 1866 Captain Andrew Sheridan, post commander, directed Ladd to reduce his prices to conform with those set by the post council of administration. Ladd was also charged with purchasing government corn from soldiers, and his store was closed until the matter was settled. Ladd was exonerated of receiving corn, and the store reopened the following day. Sheridan directed the post council of administration, as required by army regulations, to supervise the sutler's business and enforce the prices set for all commodities. The council reviewed the cost of each item and the amount for transportation, and then set the selling price to include a reasonable profit, usually between 10 and 15 percent on most items.

Ladd operated the store until he sold his interest to Theodore Weichselbaum in late 1866. Tappan and Weichselbaum were partners until May 1869, when Weichselbaum sold his interest to Charles F. Tracy of St. Louis. Tappan apparently sold his share to Tracy several months later. The records do not show how long Tracy operated the store at Fort Dodge, but he was there in November 1870 and gone by 1872.

There is considerable confusion about the traders at Fort Dodge because Congress abolished the office of post sutler in 1867. The angry response of sutlers and soldiers led to further legislation that permitted isolated posts in the West to have post traders. Then the abolition of the position of sutler was withdrawn resulting in some posts, including Fort Dodge, having both a sutler and a trader operating competing stores. All were regulated by the post council of administration.

In the spring of 1868 Robert M. Johnson applied for and received an appointment as post trader at Fort Dodge, providing competition for Weichselbaum and Tappan. Johnson expected to supersede Tappan as the sole trader at the post. When this was not allowed, Johnson sublet his appointment to John H. Coryele and William H. Vandewater of Hays City. They operated under the name Johnson & Co. for an undetermined period, but this firm was only one of three "official" traders part of that time. By 1872 the office of sutler was eliminated, and the post trader enjoyed privileges similar to those of a sutler prior to 1867.

Robert M. Wright was appointed post trader at Fort Dodge on November 12, 1868. His competition may have been the reason Tappan and Weichselbaum sold their operation to Tracy, and Wright may have caused Johnson & Co. to close that store too. The Fort Dodge trader's store was only a part of Wright's enterprises, which included freighting and contracting to supply hay, firewood, and lime for Fort Dodge. Through a partner, James Langton, he became a post trader.

Wright continued as post trader until the post was closed. He was also one of the founders of Dodge City, one of the first merchants in the

Robert M. Wright, 1840–1915, came to Kansas Territory in 1859. During the next half century he was a freighter, contractor for the army (furnishing wood, hay, and lime), stage station contractor, post trader at Fort Dodge, founder and leading merchant of Dodge City, farmer, rancher, caretaker of abandoned Fort Dodge, state legislator, and author of Dodge City, the Cowboy Capital and the Great Southwest. *He was associated with Fort Dodge in various ways from its early years to its use as the Kansas Soldiers' Home.*

new railroad town, and the leading merchant there for well over a decade. After Fort Dodge was abandoned, he served several years as custodian of the buildings and lived at the old post.

The post trader's store was a major source of alcohol for officers and men. Periodically commanding officers placed restrictions on the sale of liquor by post traders. Sometimes the commanding officers tried prohibition, as Major Henry Douglas ordered in September 1868: "All sales of Beer, liquor, Wine or anything containing Alcohol to Citizens and Soldiers are prohibited until further orders." All such efforts failed. That order, for instance, was revised two months later to permit soldiers of the garrison to purchase up to three drinks per day if they had written permission from their company commander. If liquor could not be purchased on the post, supplies were available off the military reservation.

Fort Dodge, as did every other military post, attracted a variety of camp followers who offered whiskey, gambling, and prostitutes at "ranches" just outside the military reservation. After Dodge City was established, it provided all types of recreational activities for soldiers who could leave the post, with or without permission, when they were not on duty. No matter where obtained, whiskey was the nemesis of the frontier army.

Dodge City, founded at the west edge of the military reservation in 1872 after the railroad arrived, became an important center for trade, buffalo hunters, and cattle shipment. It also offered recreation for soldiers at Fort Dodge as well as civilian residents and itinerants.

Drunkenness among officers and troops was a chronic problem. The records show that at many frontier forts more than 25 percent of the officers and men were alcoholics. The post surgeon's records reveal numerous cases of inebriation, and excessive drinking was a factor in uncounted accidents and injuries. Drunkenness was a prevalent cause of a soldier's confinement in the guardhouse, and it was frequently mentioned in charges heard by a court-martial. A number of officers and enlisted men complained that much of the work at a military post was stopped for a few days after payday because most of the troops were intoxicated. There were a few teetotalers, but only a few.

In September 1867 an incident near Cimarron Crossing was caused by excessive drinking. A wagon train belonging to José L. Perea of New Mexico Territory was stranded when Indians ran off the draft animals, and soldiers were sent to guard the train until more animals could be procured. Some of the wagons contained whiskey, and the soldiers, teamsters, and employees at the stage station became intoxicated and started fighting. A Private Smith (first name unknown), Thirty-seventh Infantry, and two employees at the stage station named Huggins and Woods (first names unknown) were killed and several others wounded. More soldiers were sent to prevent further conflict, with orders to dump the remaining whiskey.

Meanwhile, the wagon train had received more draft animals from New Mexico and proceeded west. Lieutenant Philip Reade and a detachment from Fort Dodge overtook the train near Aubry Crossing and destroyed the whiskey, including nine barrels belonging to Perea and an unspecified amount belonging to Reyes Gonzales and Salvador Armijo. Perhaps referring to the same wagon train, Major Douglas later reported that soldiers from Fort Dodge had dumped 1,354 gallons of whiskey, 40 gallons of gin, and 12 "hampers of champagne." Perea appealed to José Francisco Chávez, delegate to Congress from New Mexico Territory, for assistance. He complained, "There appears to be a lack of soldiers when we require protection or escorts, but the contrary seems to be the case, & a great many miles are travelled over out of their way in order to do us an injury." Perea filed a protest and claim against the war department for the destruction of his property without cause or compensation. Major Douglas defended his action, noting that the Mexicans had no license to retail whiskey in "Indian Country." Douglas further explained that "Escort duty in a hostile Indian Country is too important a matter to be interfered with by an illegal traffic of Whiskey, & I believed myself bound by the highest obligations of duty to put a stop to it." Perea's claim was apparently not satisfied. Douglas was one of a number of officers who complained about the problems of drunkenness in the army.

On October 28, 1868, while encamped near Fort Dodge, Captain Albert Barnitz, Seventh Cavalry, in a letter to his wife, described many of his fellow officers as "inebriates" and declared that some "are seldom sober." He continued: "there appears to be a premium offered for drunkenness in the army! Almost all the old officers drink a great deal."

Second Lieutenant Richard Taylor Jacob Jr., Sixth Infantry, was stationed at Fort Dodge during part of the winter of 1871–1872. He observed the abuse of alcohol at the post and later recalled:

> Fort Dodge had an unsavory reputation, even among army posts of that region, in those days. As no liquor was allowed to be sold at any of the posts in the Indian Territory, there was a tendency on the part of both officers and men to drink to excess just before leaving Fort Dodge for Camp Supply or Fort Sill, or immediately after arrival at Fort Dodge from those posts. This served to give Fort Dodge a reputation for carousal, dissipation and revelry that was unequalled by that of any other post on the western frontier.

One example of alcohol abuse occurred in July 1872 involving an officer and some enlisted men. Second Lieutenant Edward P. Turner, Tenth Cavalry, arrived at Fort Dodge in charge of an escort comprised of soldiers in his regiment (the officer was white and the troopers were black). Post Commander Richard I. Dodge, Third Infantry, explained what happened with Lieutenant Turner:

> I was informed that he was very drunk, had fired a pistol in the Post Traders store, ridden his horse into the soldiers billiard room, and attempted to ride into the private residence of Mr. Wright, the Post Trader. I found that he had left his wagon and mules stuck fast in the Arkansas river, and with some of his men was in the public bar-room, all drinking together, and all more or less drunk. I went to the bar-room, saw what was going on, and ordered him in arrest. He refused to obey the arrest, would not recognize my authority and said "It would take an armed party to arrest him." As he was armed and drunk enough to be dangerous, I went up to him put my arms around him, and held him while Capt. [Edward] Moale, Officer of the Day, took his pistol. There was no violence whatever used. I then attempted again to pursuade [sic] him to act sensibly and obey the arrest, when calling upon his colored soldiers for assistance, he made a violent assault upon me, striking me several times in the face with his fist. When I thought I had taken as many blows as I ought to be called upon to bear, I knocked him down with a billiard cue, and had him taken to the guard-house, where he now is. I send him to-morrow under guard of Lieut. [Sebree] Smith 6th Cavalry, to Camp Supply.

In 1880 Duane Merritt Greene, a retired officer who had served in Kansas, including Fort Dodge, with the Third Infantry and Sixth Cavalry, wrote a book about the army. He declared that drunkenness was rampant at the frontier posts and that "the blighting curse of intemperance destroys ninety per cent more of the Army than powder and ball." He claimed that some men joined the army because they were "inveterate drunkards" who were "unable to obtain employment at their trades." If they were not heavy drinkers when they joined, the pressures to consume were so powerful that few were able to resist.

Despite all steps taken to control access to liquor at the post, drunkenness remained a problem. Beer and whiskey usually were available on or off the post for those who could afford the price, typically fifty cents to one dollar for a quart of beer or twenty-five cents per drink or $1.50 per quart of whiskey. In 1880 Kansas adopted constitutional prohibition, although it was not immediately enforced. In February 1881 President Rutherford B. Hayes, who had visited Fort Dodge in 1879, banned all hard liquor from military posts. This meant that officers and enlisted men went off the post to purchase alcohol, where commanding officers had no control. The abuse of alcohol remained a serious problem in the enforcement of army discipline.

Military regulations were explicit and strict and provided for punishment by court-martial, including loss of pay and confinement in the post guardhouse, for a multitude of infractions, some serious and many trivial. The records of Fort Dodge, as well as every other military post, were filled with the proceedings of courts-martial.

Many soldiers who deserted from the army were caught. The army offered a reward for the apprehension and delivery of any deserter to military authorities. In 1868 a sergeant at Fort Dodge was escorting a deserter to the post when a band of outlaws tried to free the prisoner. The sergeant fought off the desperadoes and delivered the deserter. He was later awarded the Congressional Medal of Honor for this effort. In 1870 another deserter from Fort Dodge committed suicide when the teamsters of a wagon train attempted to capture him for the reward.

Those captured received a court-martial trial which determined guilt or innocence and fixed the punishment for those judged guilty. Fort Dodge was selected as the post for trial of many captured deserters in the region. During 1868–1869, for example, 190 sentences were handed down for desertion by courts convened at the post. The punishments included dishonorable discharge in most cases, forfeiture of all pay and allowances for a specified period, confinement and hard labor up to two years, and wearing a ball and chain for a period of hard labor.

There were many other trials for such offenses as absence without leave, sleeping while on duty, drunkenness, theft, and conduct prejudicial to "good order and military discipline," which covered a multitude of sins from insubordination to swearing. Court-martial duty occupied much of the officers' time. It was a rare soldier who escaped an appearance in court during a five-year-term of service. The soldiers' morale was depressed by the heavy-handed system of military justice and by the nonmilitary work they were required to perform.

Soldiers were recruited with the impression that they would receive food, clothing, shelter, and medical care, wear attractive uniforms, carry a rifle, learn military tactics, and fight when necessary. However, most of them discovered that life at a military post included constant periods of guard duty, fatigue duty, kitchen police, and extra duty as laborers—erecting and maintaining buildings, quarrying stone, digging latrines, loading and unloading supplies, hauling garbage, and serving as teamsters. Soldiers commonly complained that they spent more time with pick and shovel than with rifle and sword. They usually welcomed field duty because it took them away from the labors of the post.

In or out of the garrison, they also complained about the food. The soldiers were supplied only basic provisions including hash, stew, soup, vegetables (usually dried or canned, sometimes fresh if a post garden were successful), beans, bread, hardtack (dubbed "cast-iron biscuits"), salt pork, fresh beef or mutton, coffee, tea, sugar, salt, vinegar, and molasses. All items were not available at all times. Some soldiers spent a considerable portion of their pay for additional food at the trader's store, where canned goods and delicacies were usually available at a high price. Early efforts to cultivate a garden frequently failed because of insufficient precipitation or insects. Apparently no gardens were planted for several years, until Post Commander W. H. Lewis renewed the practice in 1877. He directed that a fence be erected around the plot to "keep the cattle out." Rarely did the effort provide sufficient vegetables for the garrison.

Because the commissary department procured some foodstuffs in distant markets and shipped them long distances, there were problems with deterioration and spoilage. The provisions were necessarily stored at the post for months, during which time rats, mice, and insects usually entered the commissary storehouse. This situation was improved after the railroad reached Fort Dodge. The beef cattle supplied for slaughter by civilian contractors were frequently of poor quality, and the meat was notoriously tough. Buffalo meat was substituted for beef when it was available. Buffalo were plentiful around Fort Dodge until 1873, and hunting parties were often sent out to kill a few for the mess.

Buffalo were more plentiful than firewood. Only a few trees grew along the Arkansas River, but they were available about twelve miles away on the south fork of Pawnee Fork, known as Sawlog Creek. Additional trees were found on the middle and northern branches of the Pawnee, the latter being about forty miles from the post. Most firewood was supplied by civilian contractors, but the soldiers found it necessary to supplement this in some years. A few winters that were unusually cold found the soldiers without adequate supplies and forced to ration what they had as well as search for more. In May 1874 the post bakery was closed because no firewood was available. Flour was issued to the companies in lieu of bread.

Firewood, food, shelter, and clothing were provided the troops at Fort Dodge, and the quantity and quality of these affected the comfort and health of the garrison. Leisure activities, which the soldiers had to provide for themselves, were indispensable to morale and good discipline, although some habits were harmful and destructive. Medical care and sanitation were also important to the soldiers' welfare.

9

Medical Care and Sanitation

A healthy and adequate supply of manpower was essential to the efficiency of the frontier army. The quality of medical care provided affected the morale and performance of the troops. In addition to food, shelter, clothing, and equipment, the government assumed responsibility for each soldier's medical care. The quartermaster department provided housing, equipment, and clothing; the ordnance department furnished arms and ammunition; the commissary department procured and distributed food; and the medical department was responsible for health management. Each military post had one or more surgeons and a hospital. Medical supplies were shipped to Fort Dodge from St. Louis.

The post surgeon, either a member of the army who held rank in the medical department or a civilian contract physician, was responsible for diagnosis and treatment of all ailments, emergency treatment of injuries, surgery when necessary, therapy for disabilities, examination of recruits, discharge of disabled soldiers, and the administration of the hospital and supervision of sanitation of the entire post.

The physicians oversaw daily sick call, when any soldier with a physical complaint was examined, evaluated, and treated as needed. Those soldiers who were considered able were returned to duty. Those who were ailing but not in need of hospital care were sent to quarters with prescribed remedial treatment. Those requiring closer attention were

99

admitted for further care. Soldiers incurring injuries, wounds, or acute illnesses required appropriate doctoring.

The surgeon was assisted by hospital stewards, selected from the enlisted ranks, who provided nursing care, kept patients and facilities clean, prepared and served meals to patients, and performed whatever duties the physician directed. Although the position of steward could be rotated frequently, even monthly, some stewards, at the request of the surgeon, served longer periods. M. F. O'Leary served from December 1866 to November 1868. John Crawford succeeded him and performed the duties until April 1869. The steward with the longest tenure was Thomas Hills, December 1872 to June 1876. Hospital matrons were appointed from time to time, and they worked under the direction of the physicians and stewards. The physicians and stewards were required to keep detailed records about every patient.

The post surgeon was also responsible for conducting monthly sanitary inspections of the entire post (including water supply, sewage and garbage disposal, quarters, latrines, kitchens, food, and personal cleanliness of the troops) and recommending improvements to the commanding officer. In addition he was required to record daily weather conditions, describe native flora and fauna of the area, and keep a medical history of the post.

Surgeons sometimes accompanied troops into the field, especially when engagements were anticipated. They also served on courts-martial boards, boards of survey, medical examination boards, and post councils of administration. They treated civilians, including Indians, as well as military personnel. During epidemics or the appearance of highly contagious diseases they established and enforced quarantines.

The surgeons treated a profusion of injuries and diseases. Virulent diseases, often fatal, included epidemic cholera, diphtheria, influenza, and consumption (tuberculosis). More frequent ailments were less life threatening, including a myriad of fevers, dysentery, bronchitis, common cold, boils, toothache, conjunctivitis, hemorrhoids, neuralgia, tonsillitis, rheumatism, pneumonia, scurvy, ulcers, constipation, diarrhea, and venereal diseases. Excessive consumption of alcohol affected health and well being and provided patients for the post surgeon. Inebriation was one of the reasons listed in Fort Dodge hospital records for admission and treatment. In November 1870 the post surgeon complained that liquor from the post trader's store was even being smuggled into the hospital and sold to patients and staff. The post commander directed the post sutler Charles F. Tracy and the post trader Robert M. Wright to stop the practice immediately.

Fort Dodge hospital

A number of accidents and injuries resulted from intoxication, although many were the result of carelessness with weapons, livestock, and usual activities. Common injuries included burns, broken bones, lacerations, contusions, sprains, gunshot wounds (mostly from accidents rather than battles), and, in season, sunstroke and frostbite. When baseball became a popular sport, a number of minor injuries resulted, including sprained and broken fingers. Only a few injuries were received in battle. Some soldiers suffered from exhaustion and mental stress; a few were adjudged insane and escorted to an army asylum.

Post surgeons did not change as often as most other officers at a military post, although surgeons periodically rotated from one post to another. A total of sixteen physicians served at Fort Dodge, an average of almost one per year. Of these, ten were military appointments and six were contract civilians. During some periods the post had two surgeons at the same time. The terms of total service by a physician at Fort Dodge ranged from less than two months to more than one hundred months, and the average was nearly twenty months. By contrast, forty post commanders served an average of just over five months each.

The surgeon with the longest tenure, Dr. W.A. Tremaine, served intermittently as post surgeon at Fort Dodge from December 1869 until

March 1880. He often was away from the post on field duty, to fill in briefly for a surgeon at a neighboring post, serve on a court-martial or medical examination board, or to consult on a serious case at another post. His wife died at Fort Dodge of pneumonia in January 1878, and he went on sick leave the following year. In December 1879 he was on medical leave in Chicago. Captain Jacob H. Smith, Nineteenth Infantry, was also on sick leave from Fort Dodge and staying in Chicago with his wife and daughter.

An incident occurred at a Chicago hotel, but the details were never made clear due to the military covering up any hint of scandal. A Chicago newspaper reported that Captain Smith returned from a brief trip to find Dr. Tremaine with his wife at the hotel, and Smith shot the doctor twice. Dr. Tremaine, who claimed he was treating Mrs. Smith as her physician, reportedly was wounded in one arm and lost one finger. The *Chicago Tribune* stated, "Desperate efforts were made to hush up the affair by the hotel people and the army officers on duty in the city." A reporter went to the home of army surgeon William C. Spencer, where Dr. Tremaine was taken after the incident. Dr. Spencer refused to discuss the case and told the reporter, "if you publish one word about this matter I will get even with you, remember that."

Dr. Tremaine recovered sufficiently to return to Fort Dodge late the following month. He was reported as "sick in quarters" there for two months, after which he was granted an extended leave on a certificate of disability and left the post for the last time on March 28, 1880. He was transferred from the Department of the Missouri in September 1880. He apparently recovered from his ailments, and he was promoted to major surgeon in 1882, retired in 1891, and lived until 1898. Captain Smith never returned to Fort Dodge but continued to serve in the army. He retired with the rank of brigadier general in 1902.

The medical records of Fort Dodge indicate that most of the surgeons fulfilled their responsibilities with proficiency. The success of post surgeons depended on their medical knowledge and skills and the facilities at the post hospital. The hospital contained the equipment for treatment and was one of the most important buildings at the post.

The sod hospital erected in 1865 was apparently not used for that purpose until the following year, serving as an officers' mess in the meantime. The post records show that six enlisted men were admitted to the hospital for treatment in February 1866, and it continued to be used for this purpose thereafter. The first hospital had been considered a temporary structure. Plans for a permanent hospital began during 1866, and an estimate of materials needed was submitted to the chief quartermaster of the Department of the Missouri in August 1866. Permission was granted to begin work, using stone from the quarry located about eleven miles from the post, and the employment of civilians was authorized.

It was not determined when construction began, but work was halted during the winter months and renewed in the spring of 1867. A cholera outbreak in July and August 1867 interrupted construction. A makeshift frame structure, containing three rooms and covered with board and batten siding, was erected near the post to provide care for officers suffering from cholera. The hospital was completed in 1868 and began receiving patients in October of that year. A separate frame structure was erected about seventy-five feet west of the main hospital to treat black soldiers.

The main hospital stood at the northwest corner of the parade ground. It was built of dressed stone and was one story high. It housed several rooms including a ward for twelve beds, washroom, dispensary, kitchen, dining room, bedroom for the hospital steward, office and examining room, and a storeroom. The building for black troops contained a ward for five beds and storerooms. Both buildings were heated by wood-burning stoves and lighted by candles and oil lamps. Latrines for both buildings were located approximately ninety feet to the north. At some point a dead house was built near the hospital.

The post surgeons considered the hospital too small for the case load, and their requests for more space bore results in 1873. The building originally designed for black troops was remodeled and enlarged to include a ward, steward's room, matron's room, storeroom, and post-mortem room. A bathroom was attached. A board fence was erected around the hospital complex. Periodic repairs were made to the hospital buildings as needed until the post was abandoned. In 1877 lightning rods were installed on the hospital. In 1880 a porch was added to south and east sides of the main building.

The hospital records at Fort Dodge reveal the details of admissions and treatments. The register of sick and wounded for the post, from October 1865 to October 1882, show that 991 persons were admitted directly to the hospital, 2,778 were sent to quarters under treatment, 108 were admitted to the hospital from their quarters, 15 were released to quarters from the hospital, and 1,634 received treatment and were sent to duty. This was a total of 5,526 cases, and an average of 325 cases per year for a garrison that averaged 200 men. The total number of deaths at Fort Dodge was not determined, but there were 148 interments, military and civilian, in the post cemetery in 1880, which averaged 9.9 per year. The number of soldiers who died was approximately 80, an average of 5.3 per year.

These figures were similar to the averages of all frontier military posts during the same era. According to the surgeon general's office, each year surgeons treated about 1,800 cases for each 1,000 men serving. Approximately 1,500 were treated for diseases and 250 for wounds, accidents, and injuries. Approximately 13 of each 1,000 died, 8 from diseases and 5 from injuries.

One of the citizens buried at the Fort Dodge cemetery was Dodge City's marshal, Edward Masterson, killed by a drunken cowboy on April 9, 1878. The cowboy, Jack Wagner, died the next day. Masterson's remains were moved to Prairie Grove cemetery north of Dodge City the following year. At least sixty-five citizens were interred at the Fort Dodge cemetery, some of whom had been treated at the post hospital.

The medical conditions treated at the Fort Dodge hospital reveal ailments that were most common. Records note 875 cases of diarrhea, 757 of intermittent fever, 582 of inebriation, 517 of minor wounds, 513 of catarrh, 367 of rheumatism, 233 of sprains, 219 of bronchitis, 175 of venereal diseases, 148 of tonsillitis, 89 of dysentery, and 67 cases of gunshot wounds.

The only serious epidemic at Fort Dodge was the outbreak of cholera in 1867, a disease that affected travelers on the overland trails and soldiers and civilians at most of the military posts in Kansas. During July and August there were thirty cases of cholera at Fort Dodge, seventeen civilians and thirteen soldiers. The post commander, Major Henry Douglas, was one of the first cases, and his wife and sons also were stricken. A total of twenty died at the post, including the wife of the post commander, Isadore (Issie) Bowman Douglas. She left her husband with three young boys.

Except for the cholera epidemic, the medical history of Fort Dodge was routine and effective. Diseases and injuries were treated with the best knowledge and medications available, and the post hospital served well the soldiers and citizens of the area. The post surgeons provided good care and kept the troops healthy and able to perform their duties. Medical facilities grew from a small and unstable sod hospital to a solid stone structure and other buildings. The tradition of medical care at Fort Dodge has been carried on at the Kansas State Soldiers' Home, which still occupies the old fort.

10

Abandonment and a New Mission

By the early 1880s Fort Dodge had served the purposes for which it was founded. The garrison had not been involved with Indian affairs since 1878. Military supplies for Forts Supply and Elliott, which had earlier been shipped from Fort Dodge, were being sent south from Dodge City. In November 1881 General Sheridan recommended to General Sherman that Fort Dodge be closed. Citizens and the editor of the *Ford County Globe* protested but to no avail.

On September 16, 1882, General John Pope issued the order to remove the garrison and abandon the post. The remaining troops, Company E, Twentieth Infantry, commanded by Captain William Fletcher, were directed to go to Fort Supply. They departed Fort Dodge on October 2, 1882, thereby discontinuing the post. Seven soldiers were left to complete the shipment of supplies. The Fort Dodge post office was closed. Post traders Wright and Langton moved their stock of goods to Dodge City where they closed "out their stock for less than cost price." Their partnership was dissolved on January 10, 1883. The days of the military post ended at Fort Dodge, but it was destined to be occupied by former soldiers and their families.

Everything considered worth hauling to Fort Supply was taken there. The abandoned buildings were left in charge of a custodian, who was an employee of the quartermaster department and paid seventy-five dollars per month to live at the post and guard the public buildings. James

Langton served as the first custodian from his appointment on August 23, 1882, until March 1, 1883, after which Robert M. Wright served in that position. In February 1883 officials in Dodge City and Ford County took possession of the post hospital to house smallpox patients. This apparently lasted several weeks, but no information has been located to indicate when this occupation ended.

Cattle were grazed on the military reservation, and the post was used as a corral for a few years. Wright erected a fence around a portion of the reserve, and he razed the stone sutler's store and used the stone to erect some dwellings in Dodge City. Some of the fort buildings were partially demolished for building materials and some were removed. In June 1886 the remains of soldiers buried at the Fort Dodge cemetery were removed to the Fort Leavenworth National Cemetery. Military authorities debated what should be done with the buildings of the old post and, after much consideration, recommended that the secretary of war auction the buildings to the highest bidder. That could not be done, however, without an act of Congress.

On July 5, 1884, Congress passed legislation authorizing the transfer of the buildings and remaining military reservation at Fort Dodge to the Department of the Interior for disposition. The land was to be sold at public auction, with a minimum price of $1.25 per acre as required for the Osage Trust Lands. The transfer was made on January 12, 1885, by proclamation of President Chester A. Arthur, but the reservation was not offered for disposal by the Department of the Interior until 1889, and the balance was not sold until 1906.

In 1886 the Kansas legislature requested Congress to authorize the survey and sale of the reservation as soon as possible. No action was taken. The Methodist College Association of Southwestern Kansas attempted to purchase the land containing the buildings, and a bill was introduced in Congress to provide for that. Before action was taken, the Kansas legislature requested Congress to donate the lands and buildings of the reservation to the State of Kansas to be used for a state soldiers' home. The idea of turning the abandoned fort into a soldiers' home was first introduced to the Kansas legislature by Representative George M. Hoover from Dodge City in 1883. The same appeal in 1886 resulted in changing the bill before Congress to grant the land to Kansas rather than sell it to the Methodist College Association. President Grover Cleveland signed the bill into law on March 3, 1889. The State of Kansas was required to pay $1.25 per acre to the Osage Trust fund and "establish and provide for the maintenance of officers, soldiers, sailors and marines who

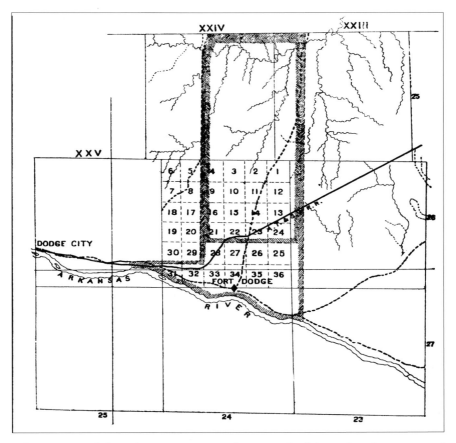

That portion of the military reservation lying north of the railroad was opened for settlement in 1880. The area containing the post buildings was transferred to the State of Kansas for the State Soldiers' Home in 1889. The remainder was sold to the public in 1906.

have served in the army, navy, or marine corps of the United States, their dependent parents, widows, or orphans, under such rules and regulations as said State may provide."

The portion of the reservation sold to the State of Kansas contained 126.7 acres. The money to pay for the land was raised by the citizens of Dodge City, and payment was made on June 13, 1889. The patent was issued to the State of Kansas. The remainder of the military reservation was sold at public auction in Dodge City on November 14, 1906.

The Kansas State Soldiers' Home was ready for occupancy on January 1, 1890, and application forms were provided to qualified persons seeking admission. The buildings that had been used by the soldiers and were still habitable for residents of the soldiers' home included the commanding officer's quarters, which served as home for the administrator, six officers' quarters, three soldiers' barracks, the hospital, two stone buildings that had served as quartermaster and commissary storehouses, and approximately twenty smaller frame structures. The old guardhouse was remodeled into a school for children of the inmates. The post cemetery became the soldiers' home cemetery.

The soldiers' home operated under a quasi-military structure. It was governed by a governor-appointed board. A commandant or superintendent was hired to administer operations. Dennis L. Sweeney was the first commandant. The primary mission of the soldiers' home was the provision of medical care, and that has remained the dominant purpose to the present. Consulting physicians were utilized in the beginning. When the number of residents increased and the need was manifest, contract physicians were hired and nurses and attendants were employed.

Only veterans and their families who were unable to care for themselves medically or financially were eligible for admission. Veterans from Kansas were given preference. The residents were required to pay what they could afford for necessities, including health care. Most of them paid 10 percent of their income for services provided.

On February 7, 1890, Andrew Prince, a Civil War veteran, became the first person admitted. He was afflicted with chronic scurvy contracted during the war. He was also the first resident to be dishonorably discharged from the soldiers' home in July 1890 for spreading scandalous rumors. His case was not unusual, however, for of the first twenty men admitted eight were dismissed within a year for disciplinary reasons, including drunkenness. Within two years the soldiers' home had 158 residents: 42 former soldiers, 34 soldiers' wives, and 82 children.

The Fort Dodge post office was reestablished in January 1893 and has continued to the present. Over the years additional land was acquired, new buildings erected, and improved hospital facilities added. The last sod building remaining from the early days of Fort Dodge was razed in 1927. A new hospital was constructed in 1928 when Fort Dodge had more than 550 residents. The road between Fort Dodge and Dodge City was paved in 1929.

Population declined during World War II, and the facility had only ninety-nine residents in 1946. In 1953 the soldiers' home was transferred to the Kansas Veterans' Commission. By 1960 the home housed 385 resi-

The two stone enlisted men's barracks at Fort Dodge were connected together, as shown here, as part of the Kansas State Soldiers' Home.

dents, and an intensive care unit was added ten years later. The tradition of medical care established by the post surgeons during the years Fort Dodge was an active military installation continues today at the Kansas State Soldiers' Home, where nearly 250 residents receive care. Several buildings of the original fort remain part of the complex at Fort Dodge.

Fort Dodge was established in 1865 to help protect the Santa Fe Trail, the railroad which replaced it, and the people who settled the region. As part of a network of military posts, Fort Dodge assisted with the restraint and removal of Indians from western Kansas. The soldiers stationed there helped bring peace to the Plains, along with the destruction of the traditional cultures of the Plains Indians.

Fort Dodge remains a part of the heritage of Kansas, and the old post lives on today as the Kansas State Soldiers' Home. Visitors are welcome at Fort Dodge where they may view some of the historic buildings, identified with handsome markers, which served the army and the nation well during the era of remarkable westward migration following the Civil War. Fort Dodge is a place where history happened, and it helped shape the society and culture of the region.

Appendix

COMMANDING OFFICERS OF FORT DODGE

An officer is listed for every month in which he served any time as commanding officer. Except for Captain Henry Pearce, who founded Fort Dodge, the officers who served during 1865 are unknown.

Captain Henry Pearce, Eleventh Kansas Cavalry, April 1865–?

Lieutenant Gilbert S. Carpenter, Eighteenth Infantry, January 1866

Captain R. L. Morris, Eighteenth Infantry, February 1866

Captain G. A. Gordon, Second Cavalry, February–August 1866

Captain Andrew Sheridan, Third Infantry, August–December 1866, November 1868–June 1869

Major Henry Douglas, Third Infantry, December 1866–October 1867, January–November 1868, March 1869

Captain William Thompson, Seventh Cavalry, August, October–December 1867

Captain John H. Page, Third Infantry, December 1867–February 1868

Lieutenant Colonel John R. Brooke, Third Infantry, June 1869–October 1870, January–February 1871

Captain Louis T. Morris, Third Infantry, December 1868–January 1869

Captain Edward Moale, Third Infantry, October 1870–January 1871, April–June 1872, October 1872–January 1873

Colonel DeLancey Floyd Jones, Third Infantry, February–October 1871

Lieutenant Colonel Daniel Huston, Sixth Infantry, October 1871–April 1872

Major Richard I. Dodge, Third Infantry, June–October 1872, January–November 1873

Captain Tullius Cicero Tupper, Sixth Cavalry, November–December 1872

Major Charles E. Compton, Sixth Cavalry, November 1873–August 1874, February–August 1875

Captain James H. Bradford, Nineteenth Infantry, August 1874–February 1875, February–March 1878, March–October 1879, August–November 1880

Captain J. Scott Payne, Fifth Cavalry, August–October 1875

Lieutenant George F. Towle, Nineteenth Infantry, October 1875–September 1876

Major William B. Royall, Fifth Cavalry, November 1875

Lieutenant John G. Leefe, Nineteenth Infantry, July–August 1876

Lieutenant Colonel William Henry Lewis, Nineteenth Infantry, March–September 1878; killed by Indians September 18, 1878

Captain Philip Halsey Remington, Nineteenth Infantry, September–October 1878

Major Henry Augustus Hambright, Nineteenth Infantry, October 1878–March 1879

Captain Emerson H. Liscum, Nineteenth Infantry, October–November 1879, May–August 1880

Major Robert Offley, Nineteenth Infantry, November 1879–May 1880

Colonel Grenville O. Haller, Twenty-third Infantry, November 1880–October 1881

Captain Thomas B. Robinson, Nineteenth Infantry, October–November 1881

Major Caleb Rodney Layton, Twentieth Infantry, November 1881–June 1882

Captain William Fletcher, Twentieth Infantry, June–October 1882

FORT DODGE MONTHLY AGGREGATE GARRISON

YEAR	JAN	FEB	MAR	APR	MAY	JUN	JUL	AUG	SEP	OCT	NOV	DEC
1865	NA	NA	NA	NA	NA	NA	NA	NA	NA	NA	NA	NA
1866	122	160	163	164	140	182	180	182	80	88	224	218
1867	229	221	216	329	325	330	315	310	371	272	352	344
1868	343	332	324	322	311	309	231	303	256	153	87	88
1869	94	93	74	147	145	155	156	149	190	223	221	249
1870	272	289	271	261	264	268	237	287	290	277	273	270
1871	266	266	265	262	257	241	215	368	215	130	187	181
1872	176	174	163	127	131	197	193	234	219	197	195	190
1873	194	201	179	315	368	366	354	371	369	178	192	237
1874	237	233	221	275	406	447	604	602	659	659	584	431
1875	328	170	164	259	173	246	416	154	95	68	159	145
1876	145	144	146	158	158	154	149	215	209	211	125	123
1877	123	122	118	118	117	75	162	98	96	107	94	90
1878	137	121	139	138	122	117	132	126	170	130	140	118
1879	114	147	147	152	147	139	137	139	136	143	144	143
1880	154	146	150	145	140	140	131	126	53	48	72	92
1881	126	127	119	112	115	113	113	107	105	52	131	127
1882	127	150	142	139	141	44	42	41	39	36		

No records have been located for 1865. The aggregate of officers and men includes those sick in the hospital, confined in the guardhouse, assigned to extra duty, and temporarily away from the post on escort or guard duty. Thus the actual number of enlisted men available for routine duty at the post was only a portion of the aggregate total.

CIVILIAN EMPLOYEES AT FORT DODGE

YEAR	JAN	FEB	MAR	APR	MAY	JUN	JUL	AUG	SEP	OCT	NOV	DEC
1865	NA	2	2	NA	NA	NA	NA	NA	NA	NA	NA	NA
1866	98	67	100	2	2	2	5	10	97	113	119	107
1867	48	11	9	121	122	235	233	248	266	214	216	204
1868	126	116	NA	9	8	61	66	77	275	NA	117	118
1869	5	5	5	134	163	NA	33	29	5	5	5	5
1870	27	14	14	14	14	17	5	4	2	2	24	25
1871	3	3	3	15	4	7	5	6	6	3	3	3
1872	3	3	3	3	3	4	4	NA	NA	22	45	45
1873	72	71	69	70	50	45	46	46	46	47	46	45
1874	43	1	1	1	1	1	58	33	47	33	35	40
1875	41	42	51	96	94	42	59	41	71	71	72	92
1876	91	89	76	47	45	60	32	32	31	31	29	16
1877	33	33	18	18	18	22	24	20	20	20	20	18
1878	21	18	15	14	14	14	14	14	30	29	15	15
1879	37	69	12	10	10	10	10	11	11	12	12	12
1880	13	14	13	11	12	13	11	11	12	12	11	12
1881	12	8	8	9	9	9	8	8	8	8	10	7
1882	8	8	8	8	8	3	3	3	3			

DESERTIONS AT FORT DODGE

YEAR	JAN	FEB	MAR	APR	MAY	JUN	JUL	AUG	SEP	OCT	NOV	DEC
1865	0	0	0	NA	NA	NA	NA	NA	NA	NA	NA	NA
1866	0	1	1	1	0	0	0	0	0	0	0	5
1867	10	7	8	0	4	6	12	4	11	1	2	7
1868	0	0	0	5	13	1	2	1	0	0	0	0
1869	1	0	0	0	1	0	0	1	0	0	1	1
1870	0	0	2	0	0	0	0	2	0	8	0	9
1871	5	1	7	2	6	6	23	3	11	0	0	3
1872	1	0	1	0	2	5	11	0	13	0	4	1
1873	0	0	8	3	18	3	4	3	7	1	1	0
1874	0	0	2	2	10	3	11	2	1	0	0	0
1875	0	0	2	1	0	0	1	2	1	0	2	0
1876	0	0	1	0	1	0	0	0	0	0	1	0
1877	0	0	2	0	3	0	5	4	1	0	0	0
1878	0	1	1	5	9	4	2	0	0	1	0	0
1879	0	0	1	2	8	1	1	1	1	1	3	0
1880	0	0	1	1	0	0	1	2	0	0	0	1
1881	0	2	4	0	0	3	2	2	3	0	0	1
1882	2	1	9	4	2	3	2	0	2	0		2

Further Reading

Berthrong, Donald J. *The Southern Cheyennes*. Norman: University of Oklahoma Press, 1963.

Carriker, Robert C. *Fort Supply, Indian Territory: Frontier Outpost on the Plains*. Norman: University of Oklahoma Press, 1990.

Haywood, C. Robert. *Trails South: The Wagon–Road Economy in the Dodge City–Panhandle Region*. Norman: University of Oklahoma Press, 1986.

Hoig, Stan. *The Peace Chiefs of the Cheyennes*. Norman: University of Oklahoma Press, 1980.

Laurence, Mary Leefe. *Daughter of the Regiment: Memoirs of a Childhood in the Frontier Army, 1878–1898*. Lincoln: University of Nebraska Press, 1996.

Leckie, William H. *The Military Conquest of the Southern Plains*. Norman: University of Oklahoma Press, 1963.

Leckie, William H. *The Buffalo Soldiers: A Narrative of the Negro Cavalry in the West*. Norman: University of Oklahoma Press, 1967.

Nye, Wilbur S. *Plains Indian Raiders: The Final Phases of Warfare from the Arkansas to the Red River*. Norman: University of Oklahoma Press, 1995.

Rickey, Don. *Forty Miles a Day on Beans and Hay: The Enlisted Soldier Fighting the Indian Wars*. Norman: University of Oklahoma Press, 1963.

Stallard, Patricia Y. *Glittering Misery: Dependents of the Indian Fighting Army*. Norman: University of Oklahoma Press, 1992.

Utley, Robert M. *Frontier Regulars: The United States Army and the Indian, 1866–1891*. New York: Macmillan Publishing Co., 1973.

Utley, Robert M., ed. *Life in Custer's Cavalry: Diaries and Letters of Albert and Jennie Barnitz, 1867–1868*. New Haven: Yale University Press, 1977.

ACKNOWLEDGMENTS

My thanks to the following individuals for their help, information, and encouragement in the preparation of this history: Betty Braddock, Joseph Byrne, David Clapsaddle, Virgil Dean, George Elmore, Thomas Railsback, David K. Strate, Dave Webb, and Timothy Zwink. The assistance and courtesy of the personnel at the following institutions was invaluable and is gratefully acknowledged: National Archives, U.S. Army Military History Institute, Kansas State Historical Society, and Kansas Heritage Center. My wife, Bonita, assisted with the research and assumed extra responsibilities so I could devote time to this project.

ILLUSTRATION CREDITS

All illustrations are from the collections of the Kansas State Historical Society, with the following exceptions: facing title page Historic General Dodge House; 19 Leo E. Oliva; 29 Cultural Heritage and Arts Center; 60 Department of the Army, U.S. Military History Institute; 62, 63 Little Bighorn Battlefield National Monument; 68 Los Angeles County Museum of Natural History; 73, 80, 81 Department of the Army, U.S. Military History Institute.

This publication has been financed in part with federal funds from the National Park Service, a division of the United States Department of the Interior, and administered by the Kansas State Historical Society. The contents and opinions, however, do not necessarily reflect the views or policies of the United States Department of the Interior or the Kansas State Historical Society.

The program receives federal financial assistance. Under Title VI of the Civil Rights Act of 1964, Section 504 of the Rehabilitation Act of 1973, and the Age Discrimination Act of 1975, as amended, the United States Department of the Interior prohibits discrimination on the basis of race, color, national origin, disability, or age in its federally assisted programs. If you believe you have been discriminated against in any program, activity, or facility as described above, or if you desire further information, please write to: Office of Equal Opportunity, National Park Service, P.O. Box 37127, Washington, D.C. 20012-7127.